Bernard Lewis, who was born in London, is the Cleveland E. Dodge Professor of Near Eastern Studies Emeritus at Princeton University. He is the author of more than two dozen books, most notably *The Arabs in History*, *The Emergence of Modern Turkey*, *The Assassins*, *The Muslim Discovery of Europe*, *The Middle East: 2000 Years of History from the Rise of Christianity to the Present Day* and, most recently, *What Went Wrong?*, which spent fifteen weeks on the bestseller list in spring 2002. His books have been translated into more than twenty languages, including Arabic, Persian, Turkish and Indonesian. His most recent work is *From Babel to Dragomans*.

*By Bernard Lewis*

The Arabs in History

The Emergence of Modern Turkey

The Assassins

The Muslim Discovery of Europe

Semites and Anti-Semites

The Political Language of Islam

Race and Slavery in the Middle East

The Middle East: 2000 Years of History from the Rise of
Christianity to the Present Day

The Multiple Identities of the Middle East

A Middle East Mosaic

What Went Wrong?

The Crisis of Islam

From Babel to Dragomans

# The Crisis of Islam

## Holy War and Unholy Terror

BERNARD LEWIS

PHOENIX

A PHOENIX PAPERBACK

First published in Great Britain in 2003
by Weidenfeld & Nicolson
This paperback edition published in 2004
by Phoenix,
an imprint of Orion Books Ltd,
Orion House, 5 Upper St Martin's Lane,
London WC2H 9EA

Fourth impression 2004

ISBN 0 75381 752 7

Printed and bound in Great Britain by
Clays Ltd, St Ives plc

*To Harold Rhode*
*in friendship*

# Contents

| | | |
|---|---|---|
| | *Maps* | XI |
| | *Introduction* | XV |
| I. | Defining Islam | 3 |
| II. | The House of War | 25 |
| III. | From Crusaders to Imperialists | 41 |
| IV. | Discovering America | 55 |
| V. | Satan and the Soviets | 71 |
| VI. | Double Standards | 89 |
| VII. | A Failure of Modernity | 97 |
| VIII. | The Marriage of Saudi Power and Wahhabi Teaching | 103 |
| IX. | The Rise of Terrorism | 117 |
| | *Acknowledgments* | 141 |
| | *Afterword* | 143 |
| | *Notes* | 147 |
| | *Index* | 153 |

# Maps

The Age of the Caliphs      xi

The Ottoman Empire      xii

The Age of Imperialism      xiii

The Middle East Today      xiv

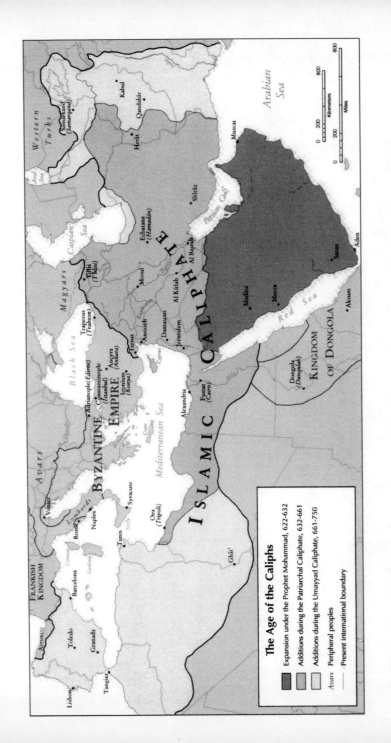

## The Age of the Caliphs

- Expansion under the Prophet Mohammad, 622-632
- Additions during the Patriarchal Caliphate, 632-661
- Additions during the Umayyad Caliphate, 661-750
- *Avars* Peripheral peoples
- Present international boundary

FRANKISH KINGDOM

BYZANTINE EMPIRE

ISLAMIC CALIPHATE

KINGDOM OF DONGOLA

*Western Turks*

*Magyars*

*Avars*

*Lombards*

*Black Sea*

*Caspian Sea*

*Aral Sea*

*Mediterranean Sea*

*Red Sea*

*Arabian Sea*

*Persian Gulf*

Lisbon
Toledo
Granada
Tangier
Barcelona
Rome
Naples
Venice
Syracuse
Tunis
Oea (Tripoli)
Ghat
Alexandria
Fustat (Cairo)
Dongola (Dunqulah)
Aksum
Adana
Saina
Medina
Mecca
Aden
Muscat
Shiraz
Al Basrah
Al Kufah
Mosul
Jerusalem
Damascus
Antioch
Tarsus
Iconium (Konya)
Ancyra (Ankara)
Constantinople (Istanbul)
Adrianople (Edirne)
Trapezus (Trabzon)
Tiflis (T'bilisi)
Ecbatana (Hamadan)
Herat
Qandahar
Kabul
Samarkand (Samarqand)
Naissus
Crete
Cyprus
Corsica
Sardinia
Sicily

0    200    400    600    800
Kilometers

0    200    400    600    800
Miles

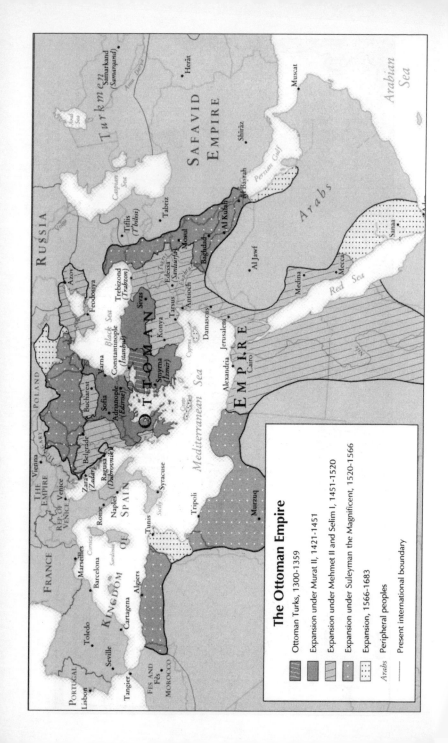

The Ottoman Empire

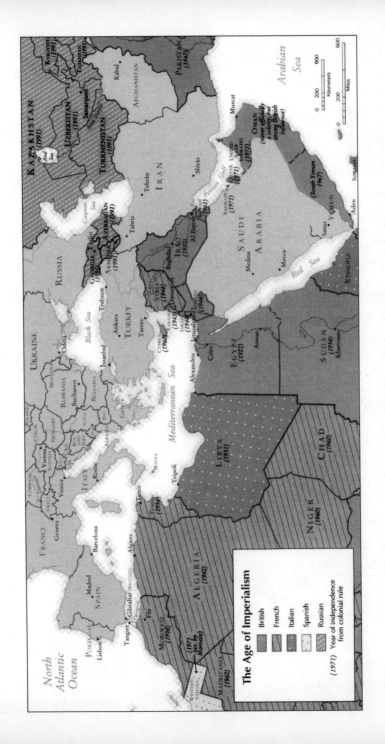

# The Middle East Today

Scale 1:21,000,000
Lambert Conformal Conic Projection,
standard parallels 12°N and 38°N

0   300 Kilometers

0   300 Miles

802840AI (R02107) 10-01

# Introduction

President Bush and other Western politicians have taken great pains to make it clear that the war in which we are engaged is a war against terrorism—not a war against Arabs, nor, more generally, against Muslims, who are urged to join us in this struggle against our common enemy. Usama bin Ladin's message is the opposite. For bin Ladin and those who follow him, this is a religious war, a war for Islam against infidels, and therefore, inevitably, against the United States, the greatest power in the world of the infidels.

In his pronouncements, bin Ladin makes frequent references to history. One of the most dramatic was his mention, in his videotape of October 7, 2001, of the "humiliation and disgrace" that Islam has suffered for "more than eighty years." Most American—and, no doubt, European—observers of the Middle Eastern scene began an anxious search for something that had happened "more than eighty years" ago, and came up with various answers. We can be fairly sure that bin Ladin's Muslim listeners—the people he was addressing—picked up the allusion immediately and appreciated its significance.

In 1918 the Ottoman sultanate, the last of the great Muslim empires, was finally defeated—its capital, Constantinople, occupied, its sovereign held captive, and much of its territory partitioned between the victorious British and French Empires. The Arabic-speaking former Ottoman provinces of the Fertile Crescent were divided into three new entities, with new names and frontiers. Two of them, Iraq and Palestine, were under British Mandate; the third, under the name Syria, was given to the French. Later, the French subdivided their mandate into two, calling one part Lebanon and retaining the name Syria for the rest. The British did much the same in Palestine, creating a division between the two banks of the Jordan. The eastern segment was called Transjordan, later simply Jordan; the name Palestine was retained and reserved for the Western segment, in other words, the Cisjordanian part of the country.

The Arabian peninsula, consisting largely of barren and inaccessible deserts and mountains, was at that time thought not worth the trouble of taking over, and its rulers were allowed to retain a precarious and limited independence. The Turks eventually succeeded in liberating their Anatolian homeland, not in the name of Islam but through a secular nationalist movement led by an Ottoman general called Mustafa Kemal, better known as Kemal Atatürk. Even as he fought—successfully—to liberate Turkey from Western domination, he took the first steps toward the adoption of Western or, as he preferred to put it, modern ways. One of his first acts, in November 1922, was to abolish the sultanate.

The Ottoman sovereign was not only a sultan, the ruler of a specific state; he was also widely recognized as the caliph, the head of all Sunni Islam, and the last in a line of rulers that dated back to the death of the Prophet Muhammad in 632 C.E. and the appointment of a successor to take his place, not as spiritual but as religious and political head of the Muslim state and community. After a brief experiment with a separate caliph, the Turks, in March 1924, abolished the caliphate, too.

During its nearly thirteen centuries, the caliphate had gone through many vicissitudes, but it remained a potent symbol of Muslim unity, even identity; its disappearance, under the double assault of foreign imperialists and domestic modernists, was felt throughout the Muslim world. Some rather halfhearted attempts were made by various Muslim monarchs and leaders to claim the vacant title, but none of them gained much support. Many Muslims are still painfully conscious of this void, and it is said that Usama bin Ladin himself had—or has—aspirations to the caliphate.

The word *caliph* comes from the Arabic *khalīfa,* which by a useful ambiguity combines the meanings of "successor" and "deputy." Originally, the head of the Islamic community was "the *Khalīfa* of the Prophet of God." Some, more ambitious, shortened the title to "the *Khalīfa* of God." This claim to spiritual authority was hotly contested and eventually abandoned, though a title expressing a similar but somewhat lesser claim, "the Shadow of God on earth," was widely used by Muslim rulers. For most of the history of the institution, the holders of the caliphate contented themselves with the more modest title *Amīr al-Mu'minīn,* usually translated as "Commander of the Faithful."

≈

Historical allusions such as bin Ladin's, which may seem abstruse to many Americans, are common among Muslims, and can be properly understood only within the context of Middle Eastern perceptions of identity and against the background of Middle Eastern history. Even the concepts of history and identity require redefinition for the Westerner trying to understand the contemporary Middle East. In current American usage, the phrase "that's history" is commonly used to dismiss something as unimportant, of no relevance to current concerns, and despite an immense investment in the teaching and writing of history, the general level of historical knowledge in American society is abysmally low. The Muslim peoples, like everyone else in the world, are shaped by their history, but unlike some others, they are keenly aware of it. Their awareness dates however from the advent of Islam, with perhaps some minimal references to pre-Islamic times, necessary to explain historical allusions in the Qur'an and in the early Islamic traditions and chronicles. Islamic history, for Muslims, has an important religious and also legal significance, since it reflects the working out of God's purpose for His community—those that accept the teachings of Islam and obey its law. The history of non-Muslim states and peoples conveys no such message and is therefore without value or interest. Even in countries of ancient civilization like those of the Middle East, the knowledge of pagan history—of their own ancestors, whose monuments and inscriptions lay around them—was minimal. The ancient languages and scripts were forgotten, the ancient records buried, until they were recovered and deciphered in modern times by inquisitive Western archaeologists and philologists. But for the period beginning with the advent of Islam, the Muslim peoples produced a rich and varied historical literature—indeed, in many regions, even in countries of ancient civilization like India, serious historical writing begins with the arrival of Islam.

But history of what? In the Western world, the basic unit of human organization is the nation, in American but not European usage virtually synonymous with country. This is then subdivided in various ways, one of which is by religion. Muslims, however, tend to see not a nation subdivided into religious groups but a religion subdivided into nations. This is no doubt partly because most of the nation-states that make up the modern Middle East are relatively new creations, left over from the era of Anglo-French imperial domination that followed the defeat of the Ottoman Empire, and they preserve the state-building and frontier demarcations of their former imperial masters. Even their names reflect this artificiality: Iraq was a medieval province, with borders very different from those of the modern republic, excluding Mesopotamia in the north and including a slice of western Iran; Syria, Palestine, and Libya are names from classical antiquity that hadn't been used in the region for a thousand years or more before they were revived and imposed—again with new and often different boundaries—by European imperialists in the twentieth century;[1] Algeria and Tunisia do not even exist as words in Arabic—the same name serves for the city and the country. Most remarkable of all, there is no word in the Arabic language for Arabia, and present-day Saudi Arabia is spoken of as "the Saudi Arab kingdom" or "the peninsula of the Arabs," depending on the context. This is not because Arabic is a poor language—the reverse is true—but because the Arabs simply did not think in terms of combined ethnic and territorial identity. Indeed, the caliph 'Umar is quoted as saying to the Arabs, "Learn your genealogies, and do not be like the local peasants who, when they are asked who they are, reply: 'I am from such-and-such a place.' "[2]

In the early centuries of the Muslim era, the Islamic community was one state under one ruler. Even after that community split up into many states, the ideal of a single Islamic polity persisted. The states were almost all dynastic, with shifting frontiers, and it is surely significant that, in the immensely rich historiography of the Islamic world in Arabic, Persian, and Turkish, there are histories of dynasties, of cities, and primarily, of the Islamic state and community, but no histories of Persia or Turkey. These names, unlike Syria or Palestine or Iraq, designate not new but old political entities, with centuries of sovereign independence. Yet until modern times even these names did not exist in Arabic, Persian, or Turkish. The name Turkey, designating a country inhabited by people called Turks and speaking a language called Turkish, seems to conform to the normal European pattern of identifying countries by ethnic names. But this name, current in Europe since the Middle Ages, was not adopted in Turkey until after the proclamation of the Republic in 1923. Persia is a European, originally Greek adaptation of the name Pars, later Fars, the name of a province in western Iran. After the Arab conquest, since the Arabic alphabet lacks a letter *p*, it came to be known as Fars. As Castilian became Spanish and Tuscan became Italian, so Farsi, the regional dialect of Fars, came to be the standard language of the country, but in Persian usage the name of the province was never applied to the country as a whole.

Both Arabs and Turks produced a vast literature describing their struggles against Christian Europe, from the first Arab incursions in the eighth century to the final Turkish retreat in the twentieth. But until the modern period, when European concepts and categories became dominant, Islamic soldiers, officials, and historians almost always referred to their opponents not in territorial or national terms but simply as infidels (*kāfir*), or sometimes by vague general terms like Franks or Romans. Similarly, they never referred to their own side as Arab or Persian or Turkish; they identified themselves as Muslims. This perspective helps to explain, among other things, Pakistan's concern for the Taliban and their successors in Afghanistan. The name Pakistan, a twentieth-century invention, designates a country defined entirely by its Islamic religion and allegiance. In every other respect, the country and people of Pakistan are—as they have been for millennia—part of India. An Afghanistan defined by its Islamic identity would be a natural ally, even a satellite, of Pakistan. An Afghanistan defined by ethnic nationality, by contrast, could be a dangerous neighbor, advancing irredentist claims on the Pashto-speaking areas of northwestern Pakistan and perhaps even allying itself with India.

References to early, even to ancient history are commonplace in public discourse. In the 1980s, during the Iran-Iraq war, for instance, both sides waged massive propaganda campaigns that frequently evoked events and personalities dating back as far as the seventh century, to the battles of

Qadisiyya (637 C.E.) and Karbala (680 C.E.). The battle of Qadisiyya was won by the Arab Muslim invaders of Iran against the defending army of the Persian shah, not yet converted to Islam and therefore, in Muslim eyes, still pagans and infidels. Both sides could thus claim it as their victory—for Saddam Hussein, of Arabs over Persians, for the Ayatollah Khomeini, of Muslims over unbelievers. The references to these battles were not detailed descriptions or narratives but rapid, incomplete allusions, yet both sides employed them in the secure knowledge that they would be picked up and understood by their audiences on both sides, even by the large proportions of those audiences that were illiterate. It is hard to imagine purveyors of mass propaganda in the West making their points by allusions dating from the same period, to the Anglo-Saxon heptarchy in England or the Carolingian monarchs in France. In the same spirit, Usama bin Ladin insults President Bush by likening him to Pharaoh, and accuses Vice President Cheney and Secretary of State Powell (named together) as having wrought greater devastation in Iraq through the Gulf War of 1991 and after than did the Mongol khans who in the mid-thirteenth century conquered Baghdad and destroyed the Abbasid Caliphate. Middle Easterners' perception of history is nourished from the pulpit, in the schools, and by the media, and although it may be—indeed, often is—slanted and inaccurate, it is nevertheless vivid and powerfully resonant.

On February 23, 1998, *Al-Quds al-'Arabī*, an Arabic newspaper published in London, printed the full text of a "Declaration of the World Islamic Front for Jihad against the Jews and the Crusaders." According to the paper, the statement was faxed to them, with the signatures of Usama bin Ladin and the leaders of Jihad groups in Egypt, Pakistan, and Bangladesh. The statement—a magnificent piece of eloquent, at times poetic Arabic prose—reveals a version of history that most Westerners will find unfamiliar. Bin Ladin's grievances as set forth in this document are not quite what many would expect. The declaration begins with an exordium, quoting the more militant passages in the Qur'an and in the sayings of the Prophet Muhammad, and then continues: "Since God laid down the Arabian peninsula, created its desert, and surrounded it with its seas, no calamity has ever befallen it like these Crusader hosts that have spread in it like locusts, crowding its soil, eating its fruits, and destroying its verdure; and this at a time when the nations contend against the Muslims like diners jostling around a bowl of food."

From here the declaration goes on to talk of the need to understand the situation and act to put it right. The facts, it says, are known to everyone and are set forth under three main headings.

First—For more than seven years the United States is occupying the lands of Islam in the holiest of its territories, Arabia, plundering its riches, overwhelming its rulers, humiliating its people, threatening its neighbors, and using its bases in the peninsula as a spearhead to fight against the neighboring Islamic peoples.

Though some in the past have disputed the true nature of this occupation, the people of Arabia in their entirety have now recognized it.

There is no better proof of this than the continuing American aggression against the Iraqi people, launched from Arabia despite its rulers, who all oppose the use of their territories for this purpose but are subjugated.

Second—Despite the immense destruction inflicted on the Iraqi people at the hands of the Crusader Jewish alliance, and in spite of the appalling number of dead, exceeding a million, the Americans nevertheless, in spite of all this, are trying once more to repeat this dreadful slaughter. It seems that the long blockade following after a fierce war, the dismemberment and the destruction are not enough for them. So they come again today to destroy what remains of this people and to humiliate their Muslim neighbors.

Third—While the purposes of the Americans in these wars are religious and economic, they also serve the petty state of the Jews, to divert attention from their occupation of Jerusalem and their killing of Muslims in it.

There is no better proof of all this than their eagerness to destroy Iraq, the strongest of the neighboring Arab states, and their attempt to dismember all the states of the region, such as Iraq and Saudi Arabia and Egypt and Sudan, into petty states, whose division and weakness would ensure the survival of Israel and the continuation of the calamitous Crusader occupation of the lands of Arabia.

These crimes, the statement goes on to say, amount to a "clear declaration of war by the Americans against God, His Prophet, and the Muslims. In such a situation, it is the unanimous opinion of the ulema throughout the centuries that when enemies attack the Muslim lands, Jihad becomes a personal duty of every Muslim."

The signatories quote various Muslim authorities and then proceed to the final and most important part of their declaration, the fatwa, laying down that "to kill Americans and their allies, both civil and military, is an individual duty of every Muslim who is able, in any country where this is possible, until the Aqsa mosque [in Jerusalem] and the Harām mosque [in Mecca] are freed from their grip, and until their armies, shattered and broken-winged, depart from all the lands of Islam, incapable of threatening any Muslim."

After citing some further relevant Qur'an verses, the document continues: "By God's leave, we call on every Muslim who believes in God and hopes for reward to obey God's command to kill the Americans and plunder their possessions wherever he finds them and whenever he can. Likewise we call on the Muslim ulema and leaders and youth and soldiers to launch attacks against the armies of the American devils and against those who are allied with them from among the helpers of Satan." The declaration and the fatwa conclude with a series of further quotations from Muslim scripture.

∾

The Gulf War of 1991, in the common Western perception, was launched by the United States and a coalition of Arab and other allies to free Kuwait from Iraqi conquest and occupation and to protect Saudi Arabia against Iraqi aggression. To view this war as an American aggression against Iraq may seem a little odd, but this perspective is widely accepted in the Islamic world. As the memory of Saddam Hussein's attack on Kuwait fades, attention is focused on the sanctions against Iraq, the American and British planes patrolling the skies from bases in Arabia, the suffering of the Iraqi people, and increasingly, the perceived American bias in favor of Israel.

The three areas of grievance listed in the declaration—Arabia, Iraq, Jerusalem—will be familiar to observers of the Middle Eastern scene. What may be less familiar is the sequence and emphasis with which these three are presented. This will be no surprise to anyone versed in Islamic history and literature. For Muslims, as we in the West sometimes tend to forget, the Holy Land par excellence is Arabia and especially the Hijaz and its two holy cities—Mecca, where the Prophet was born, and Medina, where he established the first Muslim state; the country whose people were the first to rally to the new faith and became its standard-bearers. The Prophet Muhammad lived and died in Arabia, as did his immediate successors, the caliphs, in the headship of the community. Thereafter, except for a brief interlude in Syria, the center of the Islamic world and the scene of its major achievements was Iraq, and its capital, Baghdad, was the seat of the caliphate for half a millennium. For Muslims, no piece of land once added to the realm of Islam can ever be finally renounced, but none compare in significance with Arabia and Iraq.

And of these two, Arabia is by far the more important. The classical Arabic historians tell us that in the year 20 of the Muslim era, corresponding to 641 C.E., the Caliph

'Umar decreed that Jews and Christians should be removed from all but the southern and eastern fringes of Arabia, in fulfillment of an injunction of the Prophet uttered on his deathbed: "Let there not be two religions in Arabia."

The people in question were the Jews of the oasis of Khaybar, in the north, and the Christians of Najran, in the south. Both were ancient and deep-rooted communities, Arab in their speech, culture, and way of life, differing from their neighbors only in their faith.

The attribution of this saying to the Prophet was impugned by some earlier Islamic authorities. But it was generally accepted, and it was put into effect. The expulsion of religious minorities is extremely rare in Islamic history—unlike in medieval Christendom, where expulsions of Jews and, after the Reconquest, of Muslims were normal and frequent. Compared with European expulsions, 'Umar's decree was both limited and compassionate. It did not include southern and southeastern Arabia, not seen as part of the Islamic Holy Land. And unlike the Jews and Muslims driven out of Spain and other European countries, to find what refuge they could elsewhere, the Jews and Christians of Arabia were resettled on lands assigned to them, the Jews in Syria and Palestine, the Christians in Iraq. The process was also gradual rather than sudden, and there are reports of Jews and Christians in Khaybar and Najran for some time after the decree.

The expulsion was in due course completed, and from then until now the Holy Land of the Hijaz has been forbidden territory for non-Muslims. According to the school of Islamic jurisprudence accepted by the Saudi state and by Usama bin Ladin and his followers, for a non-Muslim even to set foot on the sacred soil is a major offense. In the rest of the kingdom, non-Muslims, while admitted as temporary visitors, were not permitted to establish residence or practice their religions. The Red Sea port of Jedda for long served as a kind of religious quarantine area, in which foreign diplomatic, consular, and commercial representatives were allowed to live on a strictly temporary basis.

From the 1930s, the discovery and exploitation of oil and the consequent growth of the Saudi capital, Riyadh, from a small oasis town to a major metropolis brought many changes and a considerable influx of foreigners, predominantly American, affecting every aspect of Arabian life. Their presence, still seen by many as a desecration, may help to explain the growing mood of resentment.

Arabia was briefly threatened by the Crusaders in the twelfth century C.E. After their defeat and eviction, the next perceived infidel threat to Arabia began in the eighteenth century, with the consolidation of European power in South Asia and the appearance of European, in other words, Christian, ships off the Arabian shores. The resulting sense of outrage was at least one of the elements in the religious revival that was inspired in Arabia by the Wahhabi movement and led by the House of Saud (Arabic, Suʿūd), the founders of the Saudi state. During the period of Anglo-French influence and then domination in the Middle East in the nineteenth and twentieth centuries, the imperial powers ruled Egypt, Sudan, Iraq, Syria, and Palestine. They nibbled at the fringes of Arabia, in Aden and the Persian Gulf, but were wise enough to have no military and minimal political involvement in the affairs of the peninsula.

As long as this foreign involvement was exclusively economic, and as long as the rewards were more than adequate to sooth every grievance, the alien presence could be borne. But in recent years the terms of engagement have changed. With the fall in oil prices and the rise in population and expenditure, the rewards are no longer adequate; the grievances have become more numerous and more vocal. Nor is the involvement limited to economic activities. The revolution in Iran, the ambitions of Saddam Hussein, and the consequent aggravation of all the problems of the region, notably the Israel-Palestine conflict, have added political and military dimensions to the foreign involvement, and have lent some plausibility to the cries of "imperialism" that are increasingly heard. Where their Holy Land is involved, many Muslims will tend to define the struggle, and sometimes also the enemy, in religious terms and to see the American troops sent to free Kuwait and to save Saudi Arabia from Saddam Hussein as infidel invaders and occupiers. This perception is heightened by America's unquestionable primacy among the powers of the infidel world.

To most Americans, bin Ladin's declaration is a travesty, a gross distortion of the nature and purpose of the U.S. presence in Arabia. They should also be aware that for many, perhaps most Muslims, the declaration is an equally grotesque travesty of the nature of Islam, and even of its doctrine of jihad. The Qur'an speaks of peace as well as of war. The hundreds of thousands of traditions and sayings attributed, with varying reliability, to the Prophet and interpreted in sometimes very diverse ways, offer a wide range of guidance, of which the militant and violent interpretation of religion is one among many.

Meanwhile, significant numbers of Muslims are ready to approve, and a few of them to apply, this interpretation of their religion. Terrorism requires only a few. Obviously, the West must defend itself by whatever means will be effective. But in devising means to fight the terrorists, it would surely be useful to understand the forces that drive them.

# The Crisis of Islam

# I

## Defining Islam

It is difficult to generalize about Islam. To begin with, the word itself is commonly used with two related but distinct meanings, as the equivalents both of Christianity and of Christendom. In the one sense it denotes a religion, a system of belief and worship; in the other, the civilization that grew up and flourished under the aegis of that religion. The word *Islam* thus denotes more than fourteen centuries of history, a billion and a third people, and a religious and cultural tradition of enormous diversity. Christianity and Christendom represent a greater number and a longer period—more than 2 billion people, more than twenty centuries, and even greater diversity. Nevertheless, certain generalizations can be and are made about what is variously called Christian, Judeo-Christian, post-Christian, and—more simply—Western civilization. While generalizing about Islamic civilization may be difficult and at times in a sense dangerous, it is not impossible and may in some ways be useful.

In space, the realm of Islam extends from Morocco to Indonesia, from Kazakhstan to Senegal. In time it goes back more than fourteen centuries, to the advent and mission of the Prophet Muhammad in Arabia in the seventh century C.E. and the creation under him of the Islamic community and state. In the period which European historians see as a dark interlude between the decline of ancient civilization— Greece and Rome—and the rise of modern civilization— Europe, Islam was the leading civilization in the world, marked as such by its great and powerful kingdoms, its rich and varied industry and commerce, its original and creative sciences and letters. Islam, far more than Christendom, was the intermediate stage between the ancient East and the modern West, to which it contributed significantly. But during the past three centuries, the Islamic world has lost its dominance and its leadership, and has fallen behind both the modern West and the rapidly modernizing Orient. This widening gap poses increasingly acute problems, both practical and emotional, for which the rulers, thinkers, and rebels of Islam have not yet found effective answers.

Islam as a religion is in every respect far closer to the Judeo-Christian tradition than to any of the great religions of Asia, such as Hinduism, Buddhism, or Confucianism. Judaism and Islam share the belief in a divine law that regulates all aspects of human activity, including even food and drink. Christians and Muslims share a common triumphalism. In contrast to the other religions of humanity, including Judaism, they believe that they alone are the fortunate recipients and custodians of God's final message to humanity, which it is their duty to bring to the rest of the world. Compared with the remoter religions of the East, all three Middle Eastern religions—Judaism, Christianity, and Islam—are closely related and indeed appear as variants of the same religious tradition.

Christendom and Islam are in many ways sister civilizations, both drawing on the shared heritage of Jewish revelation and prophecy and Greek philosophy and science, and both nourished by the immemorial traditions of Middle Eastern antiquity. For most of their joint history, they have been locked in combat, but even in struggle and polemic they reveal their essential kinship and the common features that link them to each other and set them apart from the remoter civilizations of Asia.

But as well as resemblances, there are profound disparities between the two, and these go beyond the obvious differences in dogma and worship. Nowhere are these differences more profound—and more obvious—than in the attitudes of these two religions, and of their authorized exponents, to the relations between government, religion, and society. The Founder of Christianity bade his followers "render unto Caesar the things which are Caesar's; and unto God the things which are God's" (Matt. XXII:21)— and for centuries Christianity grew and developed as a religion of the downtrodden, until with the conversion to Christianity of the emperor Constantine, Caesar himself became a Christian and inaugurated a series of changes by which the new faith captured the Roman Empire and transformed its civilization. The Founder of Islam was his own Constantine, and founded his own state and empire. He did not therefore create—or need to create—a church. The dichotomy of *regnum* and *sacerdotium,* so crucial in the history of Western Christendom, had no equivalent in Islam. During Muhammad's lifetime, the Muslims became at once a political and a religious community, with the Prophet as head of state. As such, he governed a place and a people, dispensed justice, collected taxes, commanded armies, waged war and made peace. For the formative first generation of Muslims, whose adventures are the sacred history of Islam, there was no protracted testing by persecution, no tradition of resistance to a hostile state power. On the contrary, the state that ruled them was that of Islam, and God's approval of their cause was made clear to them in the form of victory and empire in this world.

In pagan Rome, Caesar was God. For Christians, there is a choice between God and Caesar, and endless generations of Christians have been ensnared in that choice. In Islam, there was no such painful choice. In the universal Islamic polity as conceived by Muslims, there is no Caesar but only God, who is the sole sovereign and the sole source of law. Muhammad was His Prophet, who during his lifetime both taught and ruled on God's behalf. When Muhammad died in 632 C.E., his spiritual and prophetic mission, to bring God's book to mankind, was completed. What remained was the religious task of spreading God's revelation until finally all the world accepted it. This was to be achieved by extending the authority and thus also the membership of the community which embraced the true faith and upheld God's law. To provide the necessary cohesion and leadership for this task, a deputy or successor of the Prophet was required. The Arabic word *khalīfa* was the title adopted by the Prophet's father-in-law and first successor, Abu Bakr, whose accession to the headship of the Islamic community marked the foundation of the great historic institution of the caliphate.

Under the caliphs, the community of Medina, where the Prophet had held sway, grew in barely a century into a vast empire, and Islam became a world religion. In the experience of the first Muslims, as preserved and recorded for

6

later generations, religious truth and political power were indissolubly associated: the first sanctified the second, the second sustained the first. The Ayatollah Khomeini once remarked that "Islam is politics or it is nothing." Not all Muslims would go that far, but most would agree that God is concerned with politics, and this belief is confirmed and sustained by the shari'a, the Holy Law, which deals extensively with the acquisition and exercise of power, the nature of legitimacy and authority, the duties of ruler and subject, in a word, with what we in the West would call constitutional law and political philosophy.

The long interaction between Islam and Christianity and the many resemblances and mutual influences between the two have sometimes led observers to overlook some significant differences. The Qur'an, it is said, is the Muslim Bible; the mosque is the Muslim church; the ulema are the Muslim clergy. All three statements are true, yet all three are seriously misleading. The Old and New Testament both consist of collections of different books, extending over a long period of time and seen by the believers as embodying divine revelation. The Qur'an, for Muslims, is a single book promulgated at one time by one man, the Prophet Muhammad. After a lively debate in the first centuries of Islam, the doctrine was adopted that the Qur'an itself is uncreated and eternal, divine and immutable. This has become a central tenet of the faith.

The mosque is indeed the Muslim church in the sense that it is a place of communal worship. But one cannot speak of "the Mosque" as one speaks of "the Church"—of an institution with its own hierarchy and laws, in contrast to the state. The ulema (in Iran and in Muslim countries influenced by Persian culture known as mollahs) may be described as a clergy in the sociological sense, in that they are professional men of religion, accredited as such by training and certification. But there is no priesthood in Islam—no priestly mediation between God and the believer, no ordination, no sacraments, no rituals that only an ordained clergy can perform. In the past, one would have added that there are no councils or synods, no bishops to define and inquisitors to enforce orthodoxy. At least in Iran, this is no longer entirely true.

The primary function of the ulema—from an Arabic word meaning "knowledge"—is to uphold and interpret the Holy Law. From late medieval times, something like a parish clergy emerged, ministering to the needs of ordinary people in cities and villages, but these were usually separate from and mistrusted by the ulema, and owed more to mystical than to dogmatic Islam. In the later Islamic monarchies, in Turkey and Iran, a kind of ecclesiastical hierarchy appeared, but this had no roots in the classical Muslim tradition, and members of these hierarchies never claimed, still less exercised, the powers of Christian prelates. In modern times there have been many changes, mainly under Western influences, and institutions and professions have developed which bear a suspicious resemblance to the churches and clerics of Christendom. But these represent a departure from classical Islam, not a return to it.

If one may speak of a clergy in a limited sociological sense in the Islamic world, there is no sense at all in which one can speak of a laity. The very notion of something that is separate or even separable from religious authority, expressed in Christian languages by terms such as *lay, temporal,* or *secular,* is totally alien to Islamic thought and practice. It was not until relatively modern times that equivalents for these terms existed in Arabic. They were borrowed from the usage of Arabic-speaking Christians or newly invented.

From the days of the Prophet, the Islamic society had a dual character. On the one hand, it was a polity—a chieftaincy that successively became a state and an empire. At the same time, on the other hand, it was a religious community, founded by a Prophet and ruled by his deputies, who were also his successors. Christ was crucified, Moses died without entering the promised land, and the beliefs and attitudes of their religious followers are still profoundly influenced by the memory of these facts. Muhammad triumphed during his lifetime, and died a sovereign and a conqueror. The resulting Muslim attitudes can only have been confirmed by the subsequent history of their religion. In Western Europe, barbarian but teachable invaders came to an existing state and religion, the Roman Empire and the Christian Church. The invaders recognized both, and tried to serve their own aims and needs within the existing structures of Roman polity and Christian religion, both using the Latin language. The Muslim Arab invaders who conquered the Middle East and North Africa brought their own faith, with their own scriptures in their own language; they created their own polity, with a new set of laws, a new imperial language, and a new imperial structure, with the caliph as supreme head. This state and polity were defined by Islam, and full membership belonged, alone, to those who professed the dominant faith.

The career of the Prophet Muhammad, in this as in all else the model whom all good Muslims seek to emulate, falls into two parts. In the first, during his years in his birthplace, Mecca (?570–622), he was an opponent of the reigning pagan oligarchy. In the second, after his move from Mecca to Medina (622–632), he was the head of a state. These two phases in the Prophet's career, the one of resistance, the other of rule, are both reflected in the Qur'an, where in different chapters, the believers are enjoined to obey God's representative and to disobey Pharaoh, the paradigm of the unjust and tyrannical ruler. These two aspects of the Prophet's life and work inspired two traditions in Islam, the one authoritarian and quietist, the other radical and activist. Both are amply reflected, on the one hand in the development of the tradition, on the other in the unfolding of events. It was not always easy to determine who was God's representative and who was Pharaoh; many books were written, and many battles fought, in the attempt. The problem remains, and both traditions can be seen very clearly in the polemics and struggles of our own times.

Between the extremes of quietism and radicalism, there is a pervasive, widely expressed attitude of reserve, even of mistrust, toward government. An example is the sharp difference, in medieval times, of popular attitudes toward the qadi, a judge, and the mufti, a jurisconsult in the Holy Law. The qadi, who was appointed by the ruler, is presented in literature and folklore as a venal, even a ridiculous figure; the mufti, established in medieval Islam by the recognition of his colleagues and the general population, enjoyed esteem and respect. A *topos* in biographies of pious men—

of which we have hundreds of thousands—is that the hero was offered a government appointment and refused. The offer establishes his learning and reputation, the refusal his integrity.

In Ottoman times there was an important change. The qadi gained greatly in power and authority, and even the mufti was integrated into the public chain of authority. But the old attitude of mistrust of government persisted, and it is frequently expressed in proverbs, folktales, and even high literature.

For more than a thousand years, Islam provided the only universally acceptable set of rules and principles for the regulation of public and social life. Even during the period of maximum European influence, in the countries ruled or dominated by European imperial powers as well as in those that remained independent, Islamic political notions and attitudes remained a profound and pervasive influence. In recent years there have been many signs that these notions and attitudes may be returning, albeit in modified forms, to their previous dominance.

⁓

It is in the realm of politics—domestic, regional, and international alike—that we see the most striking differences between Islam and the rest of the world. The heads of state or ministers of foreign affairs of the Scandinavian countries and the United Kingdom do not, from time to time, foregather in Protestant summit conferences, nor was it ever the practice of the rulers of Greece, Yugoslavia, Bulgaria, and the Soviet Union, temporarily forgetting their political and ideological differences, to hold regular meetings on the basis of their current or previous adherence to the Orthodox Church. Similarly, the Buddhist states of East and Southeast Asia do not constitute a Buddhist bloc at the United Nations, nor for that matter in any other of their political activities. The very idea of such a grouping, based on religion, in the modern world may seem anachronistic and even absurd. It is neither anachronistic nor absurd in relation to Islam. Throughout the tensions of the Cold War and after, more than fifty Muslim governments—including monarchies and republics, conservatives and radicals, practitioners of capitalism and of socialism, supporters of the Western bloc, the Eastern bloc, and a whole spectrum of shades of neutrality—built up an elaborate apparatus of international consultation and, on many issues, cooperation.

In September 1969 an Islamic summit conference held in Rabat, Morocco, decided to create a body to be known as the Organization of the Islamic Conference (OIC), with a permanent secretariat in Jedda, Saudi Arabia. This body was duly set up, and it developed rapidly in the 1970s. The OIC was particularly concerned with help to poor Muslim countries, support for Muslim minorities in non-Muslim countries, and the international position of Islam and of Muslims—in the words of one observer, the Islamic rights of man.

This organization now numbers fifty-seven member states, plus three with observer status. Two of these states, Albania and Turkey, are or aspire to be in Europe (Bosnia has only observer status); two, Surinam (admitted 1996) and Guyana (admitted 1998), are in the Western Hemi-

sphere. The rest are in Asia and Africa, and with few excep
tions gained their independence in the last half century
from the Western European and, more recently, the Soviet
empires. Most of them are overwhelmingly Muslim in population, though a few were admitted on the strength of
significant Muslim minorities. Apart from these states,
there are important Muslim minorities in other countries—
some of them akin to the majority, as in India, some of them
ethnically as well as religiously different, like the Chechens
and Tatars of the Russian Federation. Some countries, like
China, have Muslim minorities of both kinds. Many more
countries are now acquiring Muslim minorities by immigration.

There were and are important limits to the effectiveness
of the OIC as a factor in international politics. The Soviet
invasion of Afghanistan in 1979, a flagrant act of aggression against a sovereign Muslim nation, evoked no serious
protest and was even defended by some members. More
recently, the organization has failed to concern itself with
the civil wars in member states such as Sudan and Somalia.
Nor has its record in regional matters been impressive.
Between 1980 and 1988, two Islamic countries, Iraq and
Iran, fought a devastating war, inflicting immense damage
on each other. The OIC did nothing either to prevent or to
end this war. In general, the OIC, unlike the Organization
of American States and the Organization of African Unity,
does not look into human rights abuses and other domestic
problems of member states; its human rights concerns have
been limited to Muslims living under non-Muslim rule, primarily in Palestine. The OIC should not, however, be
discounted. Its cultural and social activities are important

and are growing, and the machinery that it provides for regular consultation between member states may increase in importance as the Cold War and its disruptive effects recede into the past.

Turning from international and regional to domestic politics, the difference between Islam and the rest of the world, though less striking, is still substantial. In some of the countries that practice multiparty democracy, there are political parties with religious designations—Christian in the West, Hindu in India, Buddhist in the Orient. But there are relatively few of these parties, and still fewer that play a major role. Even with these, religious themes are usually of minor importance in their programs and their appeals to the electorate. Yet in many, indeed in most Islamic countries, religion remains a major political factor—far more indeed in domestic than in international or even in regional affairs. Why this difference?

One answer is obvious; most Muslim countries are still profoundly Muslim, in a way and in a sense that most Christian countries are no longer Christian. Admittedly, in many of these countries, Christian beliefs and the clergy who uphold them are still a powerful force, and although their role is not what it was in past centuries, it is by no means insignificant. But in no Christian country at the present time can religious leaders count on the degree of belief and participation that remains normal in the Muslim lands. In few, if any, Christian countries do Christian sanctities enjoy the immunity from critical comment or discussion that is accepted as normal even in ostensibly secular and democratic Muslim societies. Indeed, this privileged immunity has been extended, de facto, to Western countries where Muslim communities are now established and where Muslim beliefs and practices are accorded a level of immunity from criticism that the Christian majorities have lost and the Jewish minorities never had. Most important, with very few exceptions, the Christian clergy do not exercise or even claim the kind of public authority that is still normal and accepted in most Muslim countries.

The higher level of religious faith and practice among Muslims as compared with followers of other religions is part of the explanation of the unique Muslim attitude to politics; it is not the whole explanation, since the same attitude may be found in individuals and even in whole groups whose commitment to religious faith and practice is at best perfunctory. Islam is not only a matter of faith and practice; it is also an identity and a loyalty—for many, an identity and a loyalty that transcend all others.

On the surface, the importation of the Western notions of patriotism and nationalism changed all this and led to the creation of a series of modern nation-states, extending across the Islamic world from Morocco to Indonesia.

But all is not as it appears on the surface. Two examples may suffice. In 1923, after the last Greco-Turkish war, the two governments agreed to solve their minority problems by an exchange of populations—Greeks were sent from Turkey to Greece, Turks were sent from Greece to Turkey. At least, that is how the history books usually tell the story. The facts are somewhat different. The protocol that the two governments signed in Lausanne in 1923, embodying the exchange agreement, does not speak of "Greeks" and "Turks." It defines the persons to be exchanged as "Turkish subjects of the Greek Orthodox religion residing in

Turkey" and "Greek subjects of the Muslim religion residing in Greece." The protocol thus recognizes only two types of identity—the one defined by being the subject of a state, the other by being an adherent of a religion. It makes no reference to either ethnic or linguistic nationality. The accuracy of this document in expressing the intentions of the signatories was confirmed by the actual exchange. Many of the so-called Greeks from the Anatolian Turkish province of Karaman spoke Turkish as their mother tongue but wrote it in the Greek script and worshiped in Orthodox churches. Many of the so-called Turks from Greece knew little or no Turkish and commonly spoke Greek—but they wrote it in the Turco-Arabic script. A Western observer, accustomed to a Western system of classification, might well have concluded that what the governments of Greece and Turkey agreed and accomplished was not an exchange and repatriation of Greek and Turkish national minorities but rather a double deportation into exile—of Muslim Greeks to Turkey, of Christian Turks to Greece. Until very recently, Greece and Turkey, both Westernizing democracies, one a member, the other an applicant for membership of the European Union, had a line for religion on their state-issued identity documents.

A second example is Egypt. There can be few, if any, nations with a better claim to nationhood—a country sharply defined by both history and geography, with a continuous history of civilization going back for more than five thousand years. But Egyptians have several identities, and for most of the last fourteen centuries, that is, since the Arab-Islamic conquest of Egypt in the seventh century and the subsequent Islamization and Arabization of the country, the Egyptian identity has rarely been the predominant one, yielding pride of place to the cultural and linguistic identity of Arabism and, for most of their history, to the religious identity of Islam. Egypt as a nation is one of the oldest in the world. Egypt as a nation-state is a modern creation, and still faces many challenges at home. At the present time, the strongest of these challenges in Egypt as in some other Muslim countries comes from radical Islamic groups, the kind now commonly if misleadingly described as "fundamentalist."

～

From the lifetime of its Founder, and therefore in its sacred scriptures, Islam is associated in the minds and memories of Muslims with the exercise of political and military power. Classical Islam recognized a distinction between things of this world and things of the next, between pious and worldly considerations. It did not recognize a separate institution, with a hierarchy and laws of its own, to regulate religious matters.

Does this mean that Islam is a theocracy? In the sense that God is seen as the supreme sovereign, the answer would have to be yes indeed. In the sense of government by a priesthood, most definitely not. The emergence of a priestly hierarchy and its assumption of ultimate authority in the state is a modern innovation and is a unique contribution of the late Ayatollah Khomeini of Iran to Islamic thought and practice.

The Islamic Revolution in Iran, like the French and Russian Revolutions which it in many ways resembles, had a tremendous impact not only at home and among its own people but also among all the countries and peoples with whom it shared a common universe of discourse. Like the French and Russian Revolutions in their days, it aroused tremendous hope and enthusiasm. Like these revolutions, it has suffered its Terror and its War of Intervention; like them, it has its Jacobins and its Bolsheviks, determined to crush any sign of pragmatism or moderation. And like these earlier revolutions, and more particularly the Russian, it has its own network of agents and emissaries striving in various ways to further the cause of the revolution or at least of the regime that is seen to embody it.

The word *revolution* has been much misused in the modern Middle East, being applied to—or claimed for— many events which would more appropriately be designated by the French *coup d'état,* the German *Putsch,* or the Spanish *pronunciamiento*. The political experience of the English-speaking peoples, interestingly, provides no equivalent term. What happened in Iran was none of these but was in its origins an authentic revolutionary movement of change. Like its predecessors, it has in many ways gone badly wrong, leading to tyranny at home, terror and subversion abroad. Unlike revolutionary France and Russia, revolutionary Iran lacks the means, the resources, and the skills to become a major world power and threat. The threat that it does offer is primarily, and overwhelmingly, to Muslims and to Islam itself.

The revolutionary wave in Islam has several components. One of them is a sense of humiliation: the feeling of a community of people accustomed to regard themselves as the sole custodians of God's truth, commanded by Him to

bring it to the infidels, who suddenly find themselves dominated and exploited by those same infidels and, even when
no longer dominated, still profoundly affected in ways that
change their lives, moving them from the true Islamic to
other paths. To humiliation was added frustration as the
various remedies, most of them imported from the West,
were tried and one after another failed.

After humiliation and frustration came a third compo-
nent, necessary for the resurgence—a new confidence and
sense of power. These arose from the oil crisis of 1973,
when in support of Egypt's war against Israel, the oil-
producing Arab countries used both the supply and the
price of oil as what proved to be a very effective weapon.
The resulting wealth, pride, and self-assurance were reinforced by another new element—contempt. On closer
acquaintance with Europe and America, Muslim visitors
began to observe and describe what they saw as the moral
degeneracy and consequent weakness of Western civilization.

In a time of intensifying strains, of faltering ideologies,
jaded loyalties, and crumbling institutions, an ideology
expressed in Islamic terms offered several advantages: an
emotionally familiar basis of group identity, solidarity, and
exclusion; an acceptable basis of legitimacy and authority;
an immediately intelligible formulation of principles for
both a critique of the present and a program for the future.
By means of these, Islam could provide the most effective
symbols and slogans for mobilization, whether for or
against a cause or a regime.

Islamic movements also have another immense advantage as contrasted with all their competitors. In the

mosques they dispose of a network of association and com-munication that even the most dictatorial of governments cannot entirely control. Indeed, ruthless dictatorships help them, unintentionally, by eliminating competing opposi-tions.

Radical Islamism, to which it has become customary to give the name Islamic fundamentalism, is not a single homogeneous movement. There are many types of Islamic fundamentalism in different countries and even sometimes within a single country. Some are state-sponsored—promulgated, used, and promoted by one or other Muslim government for its own purposes; some are genuine popular movements from below. Among state-sponsored Islamic movements, there are again several kinds, both radical and conservative, both subversive and preemptive. Conservative and preemptive movements have been started by governments in power, seeking to protect themselves from the revolutionary wave. Such are the movements encouraged at various times by the Egyptians, the Pakista-nis, and notably the Saudis. The other kind, far more important, comes from below, with an authentic popular base. The first of these to seize power and the most success-ful in exercising it is the movement known as the Islamic revolution in Iran. Radical Islamic regimes now rule in the Sudan and for a while ruled in Afghanistan, and Islamic movements offer major threats to the already endangered existing order in other countries, notably Algeria and Egypt.

The Muslim fundamentalists, unlike the Protestant groups whose name was transferred to them, do not differ from the mainstream on questions of theology and the

interpretation of scripture. Their critique is, in the b
sense, societal. The Islamic world, in their view, has
wrong turning. Its rulers call themselves Muslims and make
a pretense of Islam, but they are in fact apostates who have
abrogated the Holy Law and adopted foreign and infidel
laws and customs. The only solution, for them, is a return
to the authentic Muslim way of life, and for this the
removal of the apostate governments is an essential first
step. Fundamentalists are anti-Western in the sense that
they regard the West as the source of the evil that is corrod-
ing Muslim society, but their primary attack is directed
against their own rulers and leaders. Such were the movements which brought about the overthrow of the shah of
Iran in 1979 and the murder of President Sadat of Egypt
two years later. Both were seen as symptoms of a deeper evil
to be remedied by an inner cleansing. In Egypt they murdered the ruler but failed to take over the state; in Iran they
destroyed the regime and created their own.

~

Islam is one of the world's great religions. It has given
dignity and meaning to drab and impoverished lives. It has
taught men of different races to live in brotherhood and
people of different creeds to live side by side in reasonable
tolerance. It inspired a great civilization in which others
besides Muslims lived creative and useful lives and which,
by its achievement, enriched the whole world. But Islam,
like other religions, has also known periods when it
inspired in some of its followers a mood of hatred and violence. It is our misfortune that we have to confront part of

the Muslim world while it is going through such a period, and when most—though by no means all—of that hatred is directed against us.

Why? We should not exaggerate the dimensions of the problem. The Muslim world is far from unanimous in its rejection of the West, nor have the Muslim regions of the Third World been alone in their hostility. There are still significant numbers, in some quarters perhaps a majority, of Muslims with whom we share certain basic cultural and moral, social and political beliefs and aspirations; there is still a significant Western presence—cultural, economic, diplomatic—in Muslim lands, some of which are Western allies. But there is a surge of hatred that distresses, alarms, and above all baffles Americans.

Often, this hatred goes beyond the level of hostility to specific interests or actions or policies or even countries, and becomes a rejection of Western civilization as such, not so much for what it does as for what it is, and for the principles and values that it practices and professes. These are indeed seen as innately evil, and those who promote or accept them are seen as the "enemies of God."

This phrase, which recurs so frequently in the statements of the Iranian leadership, both in their judicial proceedings and in their political pronouncements, must seem very strange to the modern outsider, whether religious or secular. The idea that God has enemies, and needs human help in order to identify and dispose of them, is a little difficult to assimilate. It is not, however, all that alien. The concept of the enemies of God is familiar in preclassical and classical antiquity, and in both the Old and New Testaments as well as in the Qur'an.

In Islam, the struggle of good and evil acquired, from the start, political and even military dimensions. Muhammad, it will be recalled, was not only a prophet and a teacher, like the founders of other religions; he was also a ruler and a soldier. Hence his struggle involved a state and its armed forces. If the fighters in the war for Islam, the holy war "in the path of God," are fighting for God, it follows that their opponents are fighting against God. And since God is in principle the sovereign, the supreme head of the Islamic state, with the Prophet, and after the Prophet the caliphs, as His vicegerents, then God as sovereign commands the army. The army is God's army and the enemy is God's enemy. The duty of God's soldiers is to dispatch God's enemies as quickly as possible to the place where God will chastise them, that is to say in the afterlife.

The key question that occupies Western policy makers at the present time may be stated simply: Is Islam, whether fundamentalist or other, a threat to the West? To this simple question, various simple answers have been given, and as is the way of simple answers, they are mostly misleading. According to one school of thought, after the demise of the Soviet Union and the Communist movement, Islam and Islamic fundamentalism have replaced them as the major threat to the West and the Western way of life. According to another school of thought, Muslims, including radical fundamentalists, are basically decent, peace-loving, pious people, some of whom have been driven beyond endurance by all the dreadful things that we of the West have done to them. We choose to see them as enemies because we have a psychological need of an enemy to replace the defunct Soviet Union.

Both views contain elements of truth; both are dangerously wrong. Islam as such is not an enemy of the West, and there are growing numbers of Muslims, both there and here, who desire nothing better than a closer and more friendly relationship with the West and the development of democratic institutions in their own countries. But a significant number of Muslims—notably but not exclusively those whom we call fundamentalists—are hostile and dangerous, not because we need an enemy but because they do.

In recent years, there have been some changes of perception and, consequently, of tactics among Muslims. Some of them still see the West in general and its present leader the United States in particular as the ancient and irreconcilable enemy of Islam, the one serious obstacle to the restoration of God's faith and law at home and their ultimate universal triumph. For these there is no way but war to the death, in fulfillment of what they see as the commandments of their faith. There are others who, while remaining committed Muslims and well aware of the flaws of modern Western society, nevertheless also see its merits—its inquiring spirit, which produced modern science and technology; its concern for freedom, which created modern democratic government. These, while retaining their own beliefs and their own culture, seek to join us in reaching toward a freer and better world. There are some again who, while seeing the West as their ultimate enemy and as the source of all evil, are nevertheless aware of its power, and seek some temporary accommodation in order better to prepare for the final struggle. We would be wise not to confuse the second and the third.

# II

## *The House of War*

In the course of human history, many civilizations have risen and fallen—China, India, Greece, Rome, and before them, the ancient civilizations of the Middle East. During the centuries that in European history are called medieval, the most advanced civilization in the world was undoubtedly that of Islam. Islam may have been equaled—or even, in some respects, surpassed—by India and China, but both of those civilizations remained essentially limited to one region and to one ethnic group, and their impact on the rest of the world was correspondingly restricted. The civilization of Islam, by contrast, was ecumenical in its outlook, and explicitly so in its aspirations.

One of the basic tasks bequeathed to Muslims by the Prophet was jihad. This word comes from an Arabic root *j-h-d*, with the basic meaning of striving or effort. It is often used in classical texts with the closely related meaning of struggle, and hence also of fight. It is usually cited in the Qur'anic phrase "striving in the path of God" (e.g., IX, 24; LX, 1 et cetera) and has been variously interpreted to mean moral striving and armed struggle. It is usually fairly easy to understand from the context which of these shades of meaning is intended. In the Qur'an the word occurs many times, in these two distinct but connected senses. In the early chapters, dating from the Meccan period, when the Prophet was still the leader of a minority group struggling against the dominant pagan oligarchy, the word often has the meaning, favored by modernist exegetists, of moral striving. In the later chapters, promulgated in Medina, where the Prophet headed the state and commanded its army, it usually has a more explicitly practical connotation. In many, the military meaning is unequivocal. A good example is IV, 95: "Those of the believers who stay at home, other than the disabled, are not equal to those who strive in the path of God with their goods and their persons. God has placed those who struggle with their goods and their persons on a higher level than those who stay at home. God has promised reward to all who believe but He distinguishes those who fight, above those who stay at home, with a mighty reward." Similar sentiments will be found in VIII, 72; IX, 41, 81, 88; LXVI, 9 et cetera.

Some modern Muslims, particularly when addressing the outside world, explain the duty of jihad in a spiritual and moral sense. The overwhelming majority of early authorities, citing the relevant passages in the Qur'an, the commentaries, and the traditions of the Prophet, discuss jihad in military terms. According to Islamic law, it is lawful to wage war against four types of enemies: infidels, apostates, rebels, and bandits. Although all four types of wars are legitimate, only the first two count as jihad. Jihad is thus a religious obligation. In discussing the obligation of the holy war, the classical Muslim jurists distinguish between offensive and defensive warfare. In offense, jihad is an obligation of the Muslim community as a whole, and may therefore be discharged by volunteers and professionals. In a defensive war, it becomes an obligation of every able-bodied individual. It is this principle that Usama bin Ladin invoked in his declaration of war against the United States.

For most of the fourteen centuries of recorded Muslim history, jihad was most commonly interpreted to mean armed struggle for the defense or advancement of Muslim power. In Muslim tradition, the world is divided into two houses: the House of Islam (*Dār al-Islām*), in which Muslim governments rule and Muslim law prevails, and the House of War (*Dār al-Harb*), the rest of the world, still inhabited and, more important, ruled by infidels. The presumption is that the duty of jihad will continue, interrupted only by truces, until all the world either adopts the Muslim faith or submits to Muslim rule. Those who fight in the jihad qualify for rewards in both worlds—booty in this one, paradise in the next.

In this as in so many other matters, the guidance of the Qur'an is amplified and elaborated in the *hadīths*, that is to say traditions concerning the actions and utterances of the Prophet. Many of these deal with holy war. The following are a few samples.

Jihad is your duty under any ruler, be he godly or wicked.

A day and a night of fighting on the frontier is better than a month of fasting and prayer.

The nip of an ant hurts a martyr more than the thrust of a weapon, for these are more welcome to him than sweet, cold water on a hot summer day.

He who dies without having taken part in a campaign dies in a kind of unbelief.

> God marvels at people [those to whom Islam is brought
>     by conquest] who are dragged to Paradise in chains.
> Learn to shoot, for the space between the mark and the
>     archer is one of the gardens of Paradise.
> Paradise is in the shadow of swords.

The traditions also lay down some rules of warfare for the
conduct of jihad:

> Be advised to treat prisoners well.
> Looting is no more lawful than carrion.
> God has forbidden the killing of women and children.
> Muslims are bound by their agreements, provided that
>     these are lawful.[1]

The standard juristic treatises on shari'a normally contain a
chapter on jihad, understood in the military sense as
regular warfare against infidels and apostates. But these
treatises prescribe correct behavior and respect for the rules
of war in matters such as the opening and termination of
hostilities and the treatment of noncombatants and of prisoners, not to speak of diplomatic envoys.

For most of the recorded history of Islam, from the lifetime of the Prophet Muhammad onward, the word *jihād*
was used in a primarily military sense. Muhammad began
his prophetic mission in his birthplace, Mecca, but because
of the persecution that he and his followers suffered at the
hands of the pagan oligarchy ruling that town, they moved
to the town of Medina, where the local tribes welcomed
them and installed the Prophet first as arbitrator and then
as ruler. This move is known in Arabic as the Hijra, sometimes misspelt *Hegira* and mistranslated "flight." The

Muslim era dates from the beginning of the Arabian year which the Hijra took place. The first jihad was waged by the Prophet against the rulers of his birthplace and ended with the conquest of Mecca in the month of Ramadan of the year 8 of the Hijra, corresponding to January 630 of the Christian era. The Meccan leadership surrendered almost without a fight, and the Meccans, apart from those accused of specific offenses against the Prophet or a Muslim, were granted immunity for their lives and property, provided that they behaved in accordance with the agreement. The next task was the extension of Muslim authority to the rest of Arabia and, under the Prophet's successors, the caliphs, to the rest of the world.

In the early centuries of the Islamic era this seemed a possible, indeed a probable outcome. Within a remarkably short time the conquering Muslim armies had overthrown the ancient empire of Persia and incorporated all its territories in the domains of the caliphate, opening the way to the invasion of Central Asia and of India. To the West, the Byzantine Empire was not as yet overthrown, but it was deprived of a large part of its territories. The then Christian provinces of Syria, Palestine, Egypt, and North Africa were absorbed and in due course Islamized and Arabized, and they served as bases for the further invasion of Europe and the conquest of Spain and Portugal and much of southern Italy. By the early eighth century the conquering Arab armies were even advancing beyond the Pyrenees into France.

After several centuries of almost unbroken victories, the Arab jihad was finally held and repelled by Christian Europe. In the East, the Byzantines held on to the great

Christian city of Constantinople, repelling a series of Arab attacks. In the West, they began the long, drawn-out process known in Spanish history as the *Reconquista,* or Reconquest, which eventually led to the eviction of the Muslims from the territories they had conquered in Italy and the Iberian peninsula. An attempt to carry the Reconquista to the Middle East, and to recover the birthplace of Christ, conquered by the Muslims in the seventh century, was also launched. This attempt, known as the Crusades, failed totally, and the Crusaders were driven out in disarray.

But the jihad had not ended. A new phase was inaugurated, this time not by Arabs but by later recruits to Islam, the Turks and the Tatars. These were able to conquer the hitherto Christian land of Anatolia, and in May 1453 they captured Constantinople, which from then on became the capital of the Ottoman sultans, the successors of the earlier caliphate in the leadership of the Islamic jihad. The Ottomans in the Balkans and the Islamized Tatars in Russia resumed the attempt to conquer Europe, this time from the East, and for a while seemed to be within sight of success.

But again European Christendom was able to oust the invaders and again, now more successfully, to counterattack against the realms of Islam. By this time the jihad had become almost entirely defensive—resisting the Reconquest in Spain and Russia, resisting the movements for national self-liberation by the Christian subjects of the Ottoman Empire, and finally, as Muslims see it, defending the very heartlands of Islam against infidel attack. This phase has come to be known as imperialism.

Even in this period of retreat, the offensive jihad was by no means abandoned. As late as 1896, the Afghans invaded the mountainous region of the Hindu Kush in what is now northeastern Afghanistan. Until then the inhabitants were not Muslim, and the region was therefore known to Muslims as Kafiristan, "Land of the Unbelievers." After the Afghan conquest, it was renamed Nuristan, "Land of Light." During the same period jihads of various kinds were conducted in Africa against non-Muslim populations. But for the most part, the concept, practice, and experience of jihad in the modern Islamic world have been overwhelmingly defensive.

The predominantly military use of the term continued into relatively modern times. In the Ottoman Empire the city of Belgrade, an advance base in the war against the Austrians, was given the rhyming title of *Dār al-Jihād* (House of Jihad). In the early nineteenth century, when the modernizing ruler of Egypt, Muhammad 'Ali Pasha, reformed his armed forces and their administration on French and British lines, he created a "war department" to administer them. It was known in Arabic as the Divan of Jihad Affairs (*Dīwān al-Jihādiyya*) and its head as the supervisor of jihad affairs (*Nāzir al-Jihādiyya*). One could cite other examples in which the word *jihad* has lost its holiness and retained only its military connotation. In modern times both the military and the moral use of the term have been revived, and they are differently understood and applied by different groups of people. Organizations claiming the name of Jihad at the present day, in Kashmir, Chechnya, Palestine, and elsewhere, clearly do not use the word to denote moral striving.

Jihad is sometimes presented as the Muslim equivalent of the Crusade, and the two are seen as more or less equivalent. In a sense this is true—both were proclaimed and waged as holy wars for the true faith against an infidel enemy. But there is a difference. The Crusade is a late development in Christian history and, in a sense, marks a radical departure from basic Christian values as expressed in the Gospels. Christendom had been under attack since the seventh century, and had lost vast territories to Muslim rule; the concept of a holy war, more commonly, a just war, was familiar since antiquity. Yet in the long struggle between Islam and Christendom, the Crusade was late, limited, and of relatively brief duration. Jihad is present from the beginning of Islamic history—in scripture, in the life of the Prophet, and in the actions of his companions and immediate successors. It has continued throughout Islamic history and retains its appeal to the present day. The word *crusade* derives of course from the cross and originally denoted a holy war for Christianity. But in the Christian world it has long since lost that meaning and is used in the general sense of a morally driven campaign for a good cause. One may wage a crusade for the environment, for clean water, for better social services, for women's rights, and for a whole range of other causes. The one context in which the word crusade is not used nowadays is precisely the original religious one. Jihad too is used in a variety of senses, but unlike crusade it has retained its original, primary meaning.

Those who are killed in the jihad are called martyrs, in Arabic and other Muslim languages *shahīd*. The English word *martyr* comes from the Greek *martys*, meaning "witness," and in Judeo-Christian usage designates one who is prepared to suffer torture and death rather than

32

renounce his faith. His martyrdom is thus a testimony or witness to that faith, and to his readiness to suffer and die for it. The Arabic term *shahīd* also means "witness" and is usually translated "martyr," but it has a rather different connotation. In Islamic usage the term "martyrdom" is normally interpreted to mean death in a jihad and its reward is eternal bliss, described in some detail in early religious texts. Suicide, by contrast, is a mortal sin and earns eternal damnation, even for those who would otherwise have earned a place in paradise. The classical jurists distinguish clearly between facing certain death at the hands of the enemy and killing oneself by one's own hand. The one leads to heaven, the other to hell. Some recent fundamentalist jurists and others have blurred or even dismissed this distinction, but their view is by no means unanimously accepted. The suicide bomber is thus taking a considerable risk on a theological nicety.

Because holy war is an obligation of the faith, it is elaborately regulated in the shari'a. Fighters in a jihad are enjoined not to kill women, children, and the aged unless they attack first, not to torture or mutilate prisoners, to give  fair warning of the resumption of hostilities after a truce, and to honor agreements. The medieval jurists and theologians discuss at some length the rules of warfare, including questions such as which weapons are permitted and which are not. There is even some discussion in medieval texts of the lawfulness of missile and chemical warfare, the one relating to mangonels and catapults, the other to poison-tipped arrows and the poisoning of enemy water supplies. On these points there is considerable variation. Some jurists permit, some restrict, some disapprove of the use of these weapons. The stated reason for concern is the indiscriminate casualties that they inflict. At no point do the basic texts of Islam enjoin terrorism and murder. At no point—as far as I am aware—do they even consider the random slaughter of uninvolved bystanders.

The jurists insist that the spoils of war must be an incidental benefit, not a prime purpose. Some go so far as to say that if they do become the prime purpose, this invalidates the jihad and annuls its benefits, if not in this world then in the next. The jihad, to have any validity, must be waged "in the path of God" and not for the sake of material gain. There are, however, frequent complaints of the misuse of the honorable name of jihad for dishonorable purposes. African jurists in particular lament the use of the term jihad by slave raiders to justify their depredations and establish legal ownership of their victims. The Holy Law prescribes good treatment for noncombatants but accords the victors extensive rights over the property and also over the persons and families of the vanquished. In accordance with the universal custom of antiquity, enemies captured in warfare were enslaved, along with their families, and could be either sold or kept by their captors for their own use. Islam brought a modification of this rule by limiting this right of enslavement to those captured in a jihad but not in any other form of warfare.

The rules for war against apostates are somewhat different and rather stricter than those for war against unbelievers. The apostate or renegade, in Muslim eyes, is far worse than the unbeliever. The unbeliever has not seen the light, and there is always hope that he may eventually see it. In the meantime, provided he meets the necessary conditions, he may be accorded the tolerance of the Muslim state and allowed to continue in the practice of his own religion, even the enforcement of his own religious laws. The renegade is one who has known the true faith, however briefly, and abandoned it. For this offense there is no human forgiveness, and according to the overwhelming majority of the jurists, the renegade must be put to death—that is, if male. For females a lesser penalty of flogging and imprisonment may suffice. God in His mercy may forgive the renegade in the other world, if He so chooses. No human has authority to do so. This distinction is of some importance at the present day, when militant leaders have proclaimed a double jihad—against foreign infidels and against domestic apostates. Most if not all of the Muslim rulers whom we in the West are pleased to regard as our friends and allies are regarded as traitors and, much worse than that, as apostates by many if not most of their own people.

From early times, a legal distinction was made between those territories acquired by force (Arabic 'anwatan, the equivalent of the Roman jurists' *vi et armis*) and those acquired by *sulhan,* that is by some form of truce or peaceful surrender. The rules regarding booty and, more generally, the treatment of the population of the newly acquired territory differed in some important respects. According to tradition, the difference was symbolized in the mosque every Friday. In territories taken 'anwatan, the preacher carried a sword; in those taken *sulhan,* a wooden staff. The imagery of the sword remains important. To this day, the Saudi flag has two emblems set in a field of green. The one is the Arabic text of the Muslim creed: "There is no

God but God, Muhammad is the prophet of God." The other is an unmistakable representation of a sword.

In certain periods, jurists recognized an intermediate status, the House of Truce (*Dār al-Sulh*) or House of Covenant (*Dār al-'Ahd*) between the Houses of War and Islam. These consisted of non-Muslim, usually Christian, countries whose rulers entered into some sort of agreement with the rulers of Islam whereby they paid a form of tax or tribute, seen as the equivalent of the *jizya,* or poll-tax, and retained a large measure of autonomy in their internal affairs. An early example was the agreement made by the Umayyad caliphs in the seventh century with the Christian princes of Armenia. The classical example of the *Dār al-Sulh* or House of Truce was the pact agreed in 652 C.E. with the Christian rulers of Nubia, whereby they did not pay poll-tax but provided an annual tribute, consisting of a specified number of slaves. By choosing to regard gifts as tribute, Muslim rulers and their legal advisers could adjust the law to cover a wide variety of political, military, and commercial relationships with non-Muslim powers. This approach has not entirely disappeared.

∾

From an early date, Muslims knew that there were certain differences among the peoples of the House of War. Most of them were simply polytheists and idolaters, who represented no serious threat to Islam and were likely prospects for conversion. These were to be found primarily in Asia and in Africa. The major exception was the Christians, whom Muslims recognized as having a religion of the same kind as their own, and therefore as their primary rivals in the struggle for world domination—or, as they would have put it, world enlightenment. Christendom and Islam are two religiously defined civilizations that were brought into conflict not by their differences but by their resemblances.

The oldest surviving Muslim religious building outside Arabia, the Dome of the Rock in Jerusalem, was completed in 691 or 692 C.E. The erection of this monument, on the site of the ancient Jewish temple, and in the style and the vicinity of Christian monuments such as the Holy Sepulchre and the Church of the Ascension, sent a clear message to the Jews and, more important, the Christians. Their revelations, though once authentic, had been corrupted by their unworthy custodians and were therefore superseded by the final and perfect revelation embodied in Islam. Just as the Jews had been overcome and superseded by the Christians, so the Christian world order was now to be replaced by the Muslim faith and the Islamic caliphate. To emphasize the point, the Qur'anic inscriptions in the Dome of the Rock denounce what Muslims regard as the principal Christian errors: "Praise be to God, who begets no son, and has no partner" and "He is God, one, eternal. He does not beget, He is not begotten, and He has no peer" (Qur'an CXII). This was clearly a challenge to Christendom in its birthplace. A millennium later the stationing of American troops in Arabia was seen by many Muslims and notably Usama bin Ladin as a similar challenge, this time from Christendom to Islam.

To emphasize this early challenge to Christendom, the caliph, for the first time, struck gold coins, hitherto an imperial Roman prerogative. It is significant that the name of the first Islamic gold coin, the *dīnār,* is borrowed from the Roman *denarius.* Some of these coins bore the caliph's name, his title Commander of the Faithful, and the same polemical verses. The message was clear. In the Muslim perception, the Jews and later the Christians had gone astray and had followed false doctrines. Both religions were therefore superseded, and replaced by Islam, the final and perfect revelation in God's sequence. The Qur'anic verses quoted in the Dome and on the gold coins condemn what, for Muslims, is the worst of these corruptions of the true faith. There is of course an additional message, from the caliph to the emperor: "Your faith is corrupted, your time has passed. I am now the ruler of God's empire on earth."

The message was well understood, and the striking of the gold coins seen by the emperor as a *casus belli.* For more than a thousand years the struggle was waged by the caliphs of Islam from their successive capitals in Medina, Damascus, Baghdad, Cairo, and Istanbul against the Christian emperors in Constantinople, Vienna, and later, under other titles, in more distant countries farther west. Each of these, in his time, was the principal target of the jihad.

In practice, of course, the application of the doctrine of jihad was not always rigorous or violent. The canonically obligatory state of war could be interrupted by what were legally defined as truces, but these differed little from the so-called peace treaties the warring European powers signed with one another. Such truces were made by the Prophet with his pagan enemies, and they became the basis of what one might call Islamic international law. According to shari'a, tolerance of religions based on previous divine revelations was not a merit but a duty (Qur'an II, 256: "No

*other religions*

38

compulsion in religion"). In the lands under Muslim rule, Islamic law required that Jews and Christians be allowed to practice their religions and run their own affairs, subject to certain disabilities, the most important being a poll-tax imposed on every adult male. This tax, called the *jizya,* is specified in the Qur'an: IX, 29: "Fight against those who do not believe in God or in the last day, who do not forbid what God and His Apostle have declared forbidden, who do not practice the religion of truth, though they be the People of the Book [i.e., Jews and Christians] until they pay the jizya, directly and humbly." The last few words have been variously interpreted, both in literature and in practice.

Other disabilities included the wearing of distinguishing garments or badges, and a ban on bearing arms, riding horses, owning Muslim slaves, or overtopping Muslim buildings. Except for the last two and the jizya, they were not always rigorously enforced. In compensation, the tolerated non-Muslim subjects of the Muslim state enjoyed a very large measure of autonomy in the conduct of their internal communal affairs, including education, taxation, and the enforcement of their own laws of personal status, notably marriage, divorce, and inheritance. The pact or contract between the Muslim state and a non-Muslim subject community was called *dhimma,* and the members of such a tolerated community were called *dhimmīs.* In modern parlance, Jews and Christians in the classical Islamic state were what we would call second-class citizens, but second-class citizenship, established by law and revelation and recognized by public opinion, was far better than the total lack of citizenship that was the fate of non-

Christians and even of some deviant Christians in the West.

The jihad also did not prevent Muslim governments from occasionally seeking Christian allies against Muslim rivals, even during the Crusades.

# III

## *From Crusaders to Imperialists*

The Crusades figure very prominently in modern Middle Eastern consciousness and discourse, both of Arab nationalists and of Islamic fundamentalists, notably Usama bin Ladin. It was not always so.

The capture of Jerusalem by the Crusaders in 1099 C.E. was a triumph for Christendom and a disaster for the Muslims and also for the Jews in the city. To judge by the Arabic historiography of the period, it aroused very little interest in the region. Appeals by the local Muslims to Damascus and Baghdad for help remained unanswered, and the newly established Crusader principalities from Antioch to Jerusalem soon fitted into the game of Levantine politics, with cross-religious alliances in a pattern of rivalries between and among Muslim and Christian princes.

The great Counter-Crusade which was ultimately to defeat and expel the Crusaders did not begin until almost a century later. Its immediate cause was the activities of a freebooting Crusader leader, Reynald of Châtillon, who held the fortress of Kerak, in present-day South Jordan, between 1176 and 1187 C.E., and used it to launch a series of raids against Muslim caravans and commerce in the adjoining regions, including the Hijaz. Historians of the Crusades are probably right in saying that Reynald's motive was primarily economic, in other words, the desire for loot. But Muslims saw his campaigns as a provocation and a challenge directed against the holy places of Islam. In 1182, in violation of an agreement between the Crusader king of Jerusalem and the Muslim leader Saladin, he attacked and looted Muslim caravans, including one of pilgrims bound for Mecca. Even more outrageous, from a Muslim point of view, was his threat to Arabia and, notably, a buccaneering expedition in the Red Sea, involving attacks on Muslim shipping and on the Hijaz ports which served Mecca and Medina. It was these events that led directly to Saladin's proclamation of a jihad against the Crusaders—a vivid illustration of the central importance of Arabia in the Islamic perception.

The victories of Saladin and his capture of Jerusalem from the Crusaders in 1187 have long been and are today a source of inspiration to Arab leaders. Saddam Hussein refers frequently to two previous rulers of Iraq whom he claims as predecessors in his mission—Saladin, who ended the Western menace of his day by defeating and evicting the Crusaders, and Nebuchadnezzar, who dealt expeditiously and conclusively with the Zionist problem. On October 8, 2002, the prime minister of France, Jean-Pierre Raffarin, in a speech to the French National Assembly, told how Saladin was able "to defeat the Crusaders in Galilee and liberate Jerusalem." This interesting use of the word *liberate* by a French prime minister to describe Saladin's capture of Jerusalem from the Crusaders may be a reflection of present-day realignments or, alternatively, a case of extreme political correctness. In some other countries this formulation might be ascribed to ignorance of history, but surely not in France.

Even in Christian Europe, Saladin was justly celebrated and admired for his chivalrous and generous treatment of his defeated enemies. This treatment, however, did not extend to Reynald of Châtillon. The great Arab historian Ibn al-Athir explains the circumstances. "Twice, [said Saladin,] I had made a vow to kill him if I had him in my hands; once when he tried to march on Mecca and Medina, and again when he treacherously captured the caravan [bound for the Hijaz]."[1] After Saladin's great victory, when many of the Crusader princes and chieftains were taken captive and later released, he separated Reynald of Châtillon from the rest, and killed and beheaded him with his own hands.

After the success of the jihad and the recapture of Jerusalem, Saladin and his successors seem to have lost interest in the city, and in 1229 one of them even ceded Jerusalem to the emperor Frederick II as part of a general compromise agreement between the Muslim ruler and the Crusaders. It was retaken in 1244, after the Crusaders tried to make it a purely Christian city. After a long period of relative obscurity, interest in the city was reawakened in the nineteenth century, first by the quarrels of the European powers over the custody of the Christian holy places, and then by the new Jewish immigration.

The same period saw a first awakening of interest among Muslims in the Crusades, which had aroused remarkably little concern at the time they occurred. The vast and rich Arabic historiography of the period duly records the Crusaders' arrival, their battles, and the states that they established but shows little or no awareness of the nature and purposes of their venture. The words Crusade and

Crusader do not even occur in the Arabic historiography of the time, in which the Crusaders are referred to as the infidels, the Christians, or most frequently, the Franks, a general term for Catholic—and later also Protestant—European Christians, to distinguish them from their Orthodox and Eastern coreligionists. Awareness of the Crusades as a distinctive historical phenomenon dates from the nineteenth century, and the translation of European books on history. Since then, there is a new perception of the Crusades as an early prototype of the expansion of European imperialism into the Islamic world. A more accurate description would present them as a long-delayed, very limited, and finally ineffectual response to the jihad. The Crusades ended in failure and defeat, and were soon forgotten in the lands of Islam, but later European efforts to resist and reverse the Muslim advance into Christendom were more successful, and initiated what became a series of painful defeats on the frontiers of the Islamic world.

∼

Under the medieval Arab caliphate, and again under the Persian and Turkish dynasties, the empire of Islam was the richest, most powerful, most creative, most enlightened region in the world, and for most of the Middle Ages, Christendom was on the defensive. In the fifteenth century, the Christian counterattack expanded. The Tatars were expelled from Russia, and the Moors from Spain. But in southeastern Europe, where the Ottoman sultan confronted first the Byzantine and then the Holy Roman emperor, Muslim power prevailed, and these other setbacks were seen as minor and peripheral. As late as the seventeenth century, Turkish pashas still ruled in Budapest and Belgrade, Turkish armies were besieging Vienna, and Barbary corsairs were raiding both shipping and seashores as far away as England, Ireland, and, on occasion, even Madeira and Iceland. The corsairs were greatly helped in their work by Europeans who, for one reason or another, settled in North Africa and showed them how to build, man, and operate oceangoing vessels in the North Sea and even in the Atlantic. This phase did not last very long.

Then came the great change. The second Turkish siege of Vienna, in 1683, ended in total failure followed by headlong retreat—an entirely new experience for the Ottoman armies. This defeat, suffered by what was then the major military power of the Muslim world, gave rise to a new debate, which in a sense has been going on ever since. The argument began among the Ottoman military, political, and later intellectual elite as a discussion of two questions: Why had the once ever-victorious Ottoman armies been vanquished by the despised Christian enemy? And how could they restore their previous dominance? In time the debate spread from the elites to wider circles, from Turkey to many other countries, and dealt with an ever-widening range of issues.

There was good reason for concern. Defeat followed defeat, and Christian European forces, having liberated their own lands, pursued their former invaders whence they had come in Asia and Africa. Even small European powers such as Holland and Portugal were able to build vast empires in the East and to establish a dominant role in trade. In 1593 an Ottoman official who also served as a chronicler of current events, Selaniki Mustafa Efendi, recorded the arrival in Istanbul of an English ambassador. He does not appear to have been much interested in the ambassador, but he was much struck by the English ship in which the ambassador traveled: "A ship as strange as this has never entered the port of Istanbul," he wrote. "It crossed 3,700 miles of sea and carried eighty-three guns besides other weapons. . . . It was a wonder of the age, the like of which has not been seen or recorded."[2] Another source of wonderment was the sovereign who sent the ambassador. "The ruler of the island of England is a woman who governs her inherited realm . . . with complete power."

A further detail, not mentioned by the Ottoman historian, was also of some importance. The English ambassador in question was indeed formally appointed by Queen Elizabeth but was chosen and maintained not by the English government but by a trading corporation—a useful arrangement at a time when the major concern of the Western world in the Middle East was business. Indeed, it was the rapid and innovative technological and economic expansion of the West—the factory, the oceangoing cargo ship, the joint stock company—that marked the beginning of the new era. Western European ships, built for the Atlantic, could easily outperform ships built for the Mediterranean, the Red Sea, and the Indian Ocean, both in war and in commerce, and that commerce was further strengthened by two Western habits—cooperation and competition. By the eighteenth century traditional Middle Eastern products such as coffee and sugar were being grown in the new Western colonies in both Asia and the Americas and exported to the Middle East by Western merchants and corporations. Even Muslim pilgrims traveling from South and Southeast Asia to the holy cities in Arabia sometimes booked passage on European ships, since they were quicker, cheaper, safer, and more comfortable.

≈

For most historians, Middle Eastern and Western alike, the conventional beginning of modern history in the Middle East dates from 1798, when the French Revolution, in the person of a young general called Napoleon Bonaparte, landed in Egypt. Within a remarkably short time, General Bonaparte and his small expeditionary force were able to conquer, occupy, and rule the country. There had been, before this, attacks, retreats, and losses of territory on the remote frontiers, where the Turks and the Persians faced Austria and Russia. But for a small Western force to invade one of the heartlands of Islam was a profound shock. The departure of the French was, in a sense, an even greater shock. They were forced to leave Egypt not by the Egyptians, nor by their suzerains the Turks, but by a small squadron of the British Royal Navy, commanded by a young admiral named Horatio Nelson. This was the second bitter lesson the Muslims had to learn: Not only could a Western power arrive, invade, and rule at will but only another Western power could get it out.

Imperialism is a particularly important theme in the Middle Eastern and more especially the Islamic case against the West. For them, the word *imperialism* has a special meaning. This word is, for example, never used by Muslims of the great Muslim empires—the first one founded by the Arabs, the later ones by the Turks, who conquered vast territories and populations and incorporated them in the House of Islam. It was perfectly legitimate for Muslims to conquer and rule Europe and Europeans and thus enable them—but not compel them—to embrace the true faith. It was a crime and a sin for Europeans to conquer and rule Muslims and, still worse, to try to lead them astray. In the Muslim perception, conversion to Islam is a benefit to the convert and a merit in those who convert him. In Islamic law, conversion from Islam is apostasy—a capital offense for both the one who is misled and the one who misleads him. On this question, the law is clear and unequivocal. If a Muslim renounces Islam, even if a new convert reverts to his previous faith, the penalty is death. In modern times the concept and practice of *takfir,* recognizing and denouncing apostasy, has been greatly widened. It is not unusual in extremist and fundamentalist circles to decree that some policy, action, or even utterance by a professing Muslim is tantamount to apostasy, and to pronounce a death sentence on the culprit. This was the principle invoked in the fatwa against Salman Rushdie, the murder of President Sadat and of many others.

European activities in the Islamic lands went through several phases. The first was commercial expansion and, as Muslims see it, exploitation of them and their countries, both as markets and as sources of raw materials. Then came armed invasion and conquest, by which European powers established effective domination over important areas of the Islamic world—the Russians in the Caucasus and Transcaucasian lands and later in Central Asia; the

British in India; the British and the Dutch in Malaysia and Indonesia; and in a final phase, the British and French in the Middle East and North Africa. In these places the imperialists ruled for varying periods—in some, as in Southeast Asia and India, for centuries; in others, as in the Arab lands of the Middle East, for relatively short interludes.

In either case, they left their mark. In the Arab world the period of Anglo-French imperial rule began with the French in Algeria (1830) and the British in Aden (1839); continued with the British occupation of Egypt (1882), the extension of French control to Tunisia (1881) and Morocco (1911) and of British influence to the Persian Gulf; and achieved its peak with the division of the Ottoman Arab provinces of the Fertile Crescent between the two major West European Empires. This time the newly acquired territories were not simply annexed, in the traditional style, as colonies or dependencies. They were assigned to Britain and France to administer as mandatory powers, under the authority of the League of Nations, with the explicit task of grooming them for independence. This was a very brief episode, beginning after World War I, and ending after World War II, when the mandates were terminated and the mandated territories became independent. The greater part of the Arabian peninsula remained outside the imperial domains.

Nevertheless the impact of imperialism was seen as immense and, in the eyes of most people in the region, wholly harmful. The impact and the damage were both no doubt considerable, but probably less extensive and less one-sided than the nationalist mythologies would have it. There were after all some benefits—infrastructure, public services, educational systems, as well as some social changes, notably the abolition of slavery and the considerable reduction though not elimination of polygamy. The contrasts can be seen very clearly by comparing the countries that suffered under the imperial yoke, like Egypt and Algeria, with those that never lost their independence, like Arabia and Afghanistan. In Saudi Arabia universities were late and few. At the present day, for an estimated population of 21 million, there are eight universities—one more than the seven institutions of higher education established by the Palestinians since the Israeli occupation of the territories in 1967. Slavery was not abolished by law in Saudi Arabia until 1962, and the subjugation of women remains in full effect.

But there were certainly major negative consequences of imperialism and more broadly of Western or European influence, even in those countries that managed to retain their political independence, like Turkey and Iran. Notable among the effects of modernization are the strengthening of state authority by the reinforcement of the apparatus of surveillance, repression, and indoctrination, and at the same time the weakening or elimination of those intermediate powers that in the traditional order limited the effective power of autocratic rulers. Social change, and the breakdown of old social relationships and obligations, brought great harm to the society and created new and gaping contrasts, which modern communications made all the more visible. As far back as 1832, an acute British observer, a young naval officer called Adolphus Slade, noted this difference between what he called the old nobility and the new nobility.[3] The old nobility, he said, lived on their estates. For the new nobility, the state was their estate. This remains true in much of the region today.

By the early twentieth century—although a precarious independence was retained by Turkey and Iran and by some remoter countries like Afghanistan, which at that time did not seem worth the trouble of invading—almost the entire Muslim world had been incorporated into the four European empires of Britain, France, Russia, and the Netherlands. Middle Eastern governments and factions were forced to learn how to play these mighty rivals off against one another. For a time, they played the game with some success. Since the Western allies—Britain and France and then the United States—effectively dominated the region, Middle Eastern resisters naturally looked to those allies' enemies for support. In the Second World War, they turned to Germany; in the Cold War, to the Soviet Union.

As early as 1914, Germany, then allied with the Ottoman Empire, tried to mobilize religious feeling among the Muslim subjects of the British, French, and Russian Empires against their imperial masters and therefore in favor of Germany. The effort produced meager results and was effectively ridiculed by the great Dutch orientalist Snouck Hurgronje in a famous article entitled "Holy War: Made in Germany."[4]

Where the Kaiser had failed, Hitler was for a while remarkably successful. In late March 1933, within weeks of Hitler's accession to power, the Mufti of Jerusalem, Hajj Amin al-Husseini, approached the German consul-general in Jerusalem, Dr. Heinrich Wolff, and offered his services. The consul, reporting this offer to Berlin, recommended that it be rejected or at least disregarded. As long as there was any hope of winning over the British Empire as an ally of Germany, there was no point in antagonizing the British by forming links with what was then a primarily anti-British movement. It was not until after the Munich Agreements in 1938, when Hitler finally gave up hope of recruiting the British into an Aryan alliance with Germany, that the overtures of the Palestinian leadership were accepted. From then on and throughout the war years their links were very close, and the mufti, in Jerusalem, then Beirut, then Baghdad, and finally from his office on the outskirts of Berlin, played a significant role in inter-Arab politics. In 1941, with German help via Vichy-controlled Syria, Rashid 'Ali succeeded for a while in establishing a pro-Axis regime in Iraq. He was defeated by Allied troops and fled to Germany. Even Anwar Sadat, by his own admission, worked as a German spy in British-occupied Egypt.[5]

The defeat and collapse of the Third Reich and its various agencies left an aching void. As many saw it, it was during the resulting interlude that in 1948 the Jews were able to set up their state and inflict a humiliating defeat on the Arab armies that were sent to prevent it. A new patron and protector, a replacement for the Third Reich, was urgently needed. It was found in the Soviet Union.

And then came the collapse of the Soviet Union, which left the United States as the sole world superpower. The era of Middle Eastern history that had been inaugurated by Bonaparte and Nelson was ended by Mikhail Gorbachev and the elder George Bush. At first, it seemed that the era of imperial rivalry had ended with the withdrawal of both rivals—the Soviet Union because it couldn't, the United States because it wouldn't play the imperial role. But before long events, notably the Iranian Revolution and the wars of the Iraqi dictator Saddam Hussein, forced the United States to involve itself more directly in the affairs of the region. Middle Easterners saw this as a new phase in the old imperial game. Americans did not, and showed that they had neither the desire nor the aptitude for an imperial role.

Muslim leaders, both in government and in opposition, reacted in different ways to this new situation. For some, the natural response was to seek a new patron—a successor to the Third Reich and the Soviet Union, to whom they might turn for encouragement, support, and help in the war against the West. The West as a power bloc had meanwhile moved farther west and now consisted essentially of the United States, leaving an interesting new possibility for continental Europe to assume the opposing role. Some Europeans indeed, sharing for reasons of their own the rancor and hostility of the Middle East toward the United States, have shown willingness to accept this role. But though they may have the will, they lack the means.

The collapse of the Soviet Union, followed by the defeat of Saddam Hussein in the Gulf War of 1991, was a devastating blow to secular nationalist movements, notably that of the Palestinians, who once again, as in 1945, found themselves bereft of a great power patron and helper in their cause. Their Soviet protector was gone. Even their Arab financial backers in Kuwait and Saudi Arabia, angered by enthusiastic Palestinian support for Saddam Hussein, for a while stopped their subsidies, leaving the Palestinians isolated, impoverished, and enfeebled. It was this situation that forced them to think the unthinkable and enter into a peace process with Israel. The PLO was rescued, in fundamentalist eyes ignominiously, by the

Americans and the Israelis, and induced to enter into a demeaning dialogue with Israel.

All this gave greater plausibility to the fundamentalists' view of the world, and greater appeal to their case. They—and notably Usama bin Ladin—interpreted the collapse of the Soviet Union in a different way. In their perception it was they, not America, that had won the Cold War. In their eyes, the Soviet Union was not the benign helper in the common struggle against the Jews and the Western imperialists but rather the fountainhead of atheism and unbelief, the oppressor of many millions of Muslim subjects, and the invader of Afghanistan. As they saw it, not implausibly, it was their struggle in Afghanistan that had defeated the mighty Red Army and driven the Soviets to defeat and collapse. Having disposed of the more ferocious and more dangerous of the two infidel superpowers, their next task was to deal with the other, the United States, and in this war the compromisers were tools and agents of the infidel enemy. For a variety of reasons, the Islamic fundamentalists believed that fighting America would be a simpler and easier task. In their view, the United States had become morally corrupt, socially degenerate, and in consequence, politically and militarily enfeebled. This perception has an interesting history.

# IV

## *Discovering America*

For a long time, remarkably little was known about
America in the lands of Islam. At first, the voyages of discovery aroused some interest—the only surviving copy of
Christopher Columbus's own map of America is a Turkish
translation and adaptation, still preserved in the Topkapi
Palace Museum in Istanbul. A sixteenth-century Turkish
geographer's account of the discovery of the New World,
entitled *The History of Western India*, was one of the first
books printed in Turkey—in the eighteenth century. But
interest was minimal, and not much was said about
America in Turkish, Arabic, or other Muslim languages
until a relatively late date. The American Revolution,
unlike the French Revolution a few years later, passed
almost unnoticed and was seen, if at all, as a familiar type
of insurrection. A Moroccan ambassador who was in Spain
at the time wrote what must surely be the first Arabic
account of the American Revolution:

> The English Ambassador left Spain because of the war
> that broke out between the Spaniards and the English.
> The cause of this was that the people of America were
> subjects of the English king and thanks to the revenue
> which he collected from them he was stronger than all

the other Christian peoples. It is said that he increased the burden of taxes and imposts upon them, and sent them a ship laden with tea and compelled them to pay for it more than was customary. This they refused and they asked him to accept the money that was due to him from them but not to impose excessive taxes on them. This he refused and they rose in rebellion against him, seeking independence. The French helped them in their rebellion against the English, hoping in this way to injure and weaken the English king because he was the strongest of the different races of Christians on the sea.[1]

The sultan of Morocco signed a treaty of friendship with the United States in 1787, and thereafter the new republic had a number of dealings, some friendly, some hostile, mostly commercial, all of them limited, with other Muslim states.

The first recorded mention of America as a political symbol in the Islamic world was in Istanbul on July 14, 1793, when the newly arrived ambassador of the French Republic held a public celebration culminating in a salute of guns from two French ships moored at Seraglio point. According to the ambassador's report, they hoisted the colors of the Ottoman Empire, of the French and American Republics, and "those of a few other powers who had not soiled their arms in the impious league of tyrants."[2] A subsequent French ambassador in Istanbul, General Aubert du Bayet, (later Dubayet), who arrived in 1796, was himself in a sense an American, having been born in New Orleans and fought in the army of the United States. He devoted some effort to spreading the ideas of the revolution in Turkey.

But these were French, not American enterprises, and while the ideas of the French Revolution reverberated in Turkish, Arabic, and other thought and letters through the nineteenth century, the American Revolution, and the American Republic to which it gave birth, for long remained unnoticed and even unknown. Even the growing American presence—merchants, consuls, missionaries, and teachers—aroused little or no curiosity, and is almost unmentioned in the literature and the newspapers of the time. Textbooks of geography, mostly translated or adapted from European originals, include brief factual accounts of the Western Hemisphere; the newspapers include a few scattered references to events in the United States, usually referred to by a form of its French name, *États Unis,* in Arabic *Itāzūnī* or something of the sort. A school textbook published in Egypt in 1833, translated from French and adapted by the famous writer and translator Sheikh Rifāʿa Rāfiʿ al-Tahtāwī (1801–1873) adds a brief description of the *Itāzūnī* "as a state (*dawla*) composed of several regions (*iqlīm*), assembled in one republic in the land of North America. Its inhabitants are tribes who came . . . from England and took possession of that land. Then they freed themselves from the grasp of the English and became free and independent on their own. This country is among the greatest civilized countries in America, and in it worship in all faiths and religious communities is permitted. The seat of its government is a town called Washington."[3] The concluding sentences are remarkable.

In the late nineteenth and early twentieth centuries, somewhat more attention is given to America in textbooks and encyclopedias on the one hand and newspapers on the other, but it is still very limited, and seems to have been in the main confined to the non-Muslim minorities. References to America in the general literature area are on the whole neither positive nor negative but briefly descriptive. Missionaries were of course not liked in Muslim circles, but otherwise there seems to have been no mistrust, still less hatred. After the end of the Civil War, some unemployed American officers even found careers in the service of Muslim rulers, helping them to modernize their armies. American missionaries, though forbidden to proselytize Muslims, were able to turn some Orthodox Christians into Presbyterians and, more important, to provide modern secondary and higher education to growing numbers of boys and later girls, at first from the minorities, eventually from among the Muslims. Some of the graduates of these schools even went to the United States, to continue their education in American colleges and universities. These too, to begin with, came mainly from Christian minorities; they were followed in due course by increasing numbers of their Muslim compatriots, some of them even funded by the governments of their countries.

The Second World War, the oil industry, and postwar developments brought many Americans to the Islamic lands; increasing numbers of Muslims also came to America, at first as students, then as teachers, businessmen, or other visitors, eventually as immigrants. Cinema and later television brought the American way of life, or at any rate a certain version of it, before countless millions to whom the very name of America had previously been meaningless or unknown. A wide range of American products, particularly in the immediate postwar years, when

European competition was virtually eliminated and Japanese competition had not yet arisen, reached into the remotest markets of the Muslim world, winning new customers and, perhaps more important, creating new tastes and ambitions. For some, America represented freedom and justice and opportunity. For many more, it represented wealth and power and success, at a time when these qualities were not regarded as sins or crimes.

And then came the great change, when the leaders of a widespread and widening religious revival sought out and identified their enemies as the enemies of God, and gave them "a local habitation and a name" in the Western Hemisphere. Suddenly, or so it seemed, America had become the archenemy, the incarnation of evil, the diabolic opponent of all that is good, and specifically, for Muslims, of Islam. Why?

∼

Among the components in the mood of anti-Americanism were certain intellectual influences coming from Europe. One of these was from Germany, where a negative view of America formed part of a school of thought, including writers as diverse as Rainer Maria Rilke, Oswald Spengler, Ernst Jünger, and Martin Heidegger. In this perception, America was the ultimate example of civilization without culture; rich and comfortable, materially advanced but soulless and artificial; assembled or at best constructed, not grown; mechanical not organic; technologically complex but without the spirituality and vitality of the rooted, human, national cultures of the Germans and other "authentic" peoples. German philosophy and particularly the philosophy of education enjoyed a considerable vogue among Arab and some other Muslim intellectuals in the 1930s and early 1940s, and this philosophic anti-Americanism was part of the message. The Nazi version of German ideologies was influential in nationalist circles, notably among the founders and followers of the Ba'th Party in Syria and Iraq. After the French surrender to Germany in June 1940, the French mandated territories of Syria and Lebanon remained under the control of the Vichy authorities and were therefore readily accessible to the Germans, serving as a base for their activities in the Arab world. Notable among these was the attempt—for a while successful—to establish a pro-Nazi regime in Iraq. The foundation of the Ba'th Party dates from this period. These activities ended with the British (and Free French) occupation of Syria-Lebanon in July 1941, but the Ba'th Party and its distinctive ideologies survived.

The theme of American artificiality and lack of a genuine national identity like that of the Arabs occurs frequently in the writings of the Ba'th Party and is occasionally invoked by Saddam Hussein, for example in a speech of January 2002. As the wars—the Second World War, then the Cold War—continued, and American leadership of the West became more obvious, the American share of the resulting hatred became more significant.

After the collapse of the Third Reich and the ending of German influence, another power and another philosophy, even more anti-American, took its place—the Soviet version of Marxism, with its denunciation of Western capitalism, and of America as its most advanced and dangerous form. The fact that the Russians ruled, with no light hand, over the vast Asian empire conquered by the czars and reconquered by the Soviets did not prevent them from posing, with considerable success, as the champions and sponsors of the anti-imperialist movements that swept through the world after World War II, notably but not exclusively in the Middle East. In 1945, so it seemed at the time, socialism was the wave of the future. In Eastern Europe, the Soviet Union had triumphed on the battlefield. In Western Europe, the British Labor Party defeated even the great Winston Churchill in the general election of 1945. Various forms of socialism were eagerly embraced by governments and movements all over the Arab world.

But though these foreign sponsors and imported philosophies provided material help and intellectual expression for anti-Westernism and anti-Americanism, they did not cause it, and certainly they do not explain the widespread anti-Westernism that made so many, in the Middle East and elsewhere in the Islamic world, receptive to such ideas. It must surely be clear that what won support for such totally diverse doctrines was not Nazi race theory, which can have had little appeal for Arabs, or Soviet atheist Communism, which has no appeal for Muslims, but rather their basic anti-Westernism. Nazism and Communism were the main forces opposed to the West, both as a way of life and as a power in the world, and as such they could count on the sympathy or even the collaboration of those who saw in the West their principal enemy.

But why? If we turn from the general to the specific, there is no lack of individual policies and actions, pursued and taken by individual Western governments, that have aroused the passionate anger of Middle Eastern and other Islamic peoples, expressed in their various struggles—to win independence from foreign rule or domination; to free resources, notably oil, from foreign exploitation; to oust rulers and regimes seen as agents or imitators of the West. Yet all too often, when these policies are abandoned and the problems resolved, there is at best only a local and temporary alleviation. The British left Egypt, the French left Algeria, both left their other Arab possessions, the monarchies were overthrown in Iraq and in Egypt, the westernizing shah left Iran, the Western oil companies relinquished control of the oil wells that they had discovered and developed, and contented themselves with the best arrangements they could make with the governments of these countries—yet the generalized resentment of the fundamentalists and other extremists against the West remains and grows and is not appeased.

~

Perhaps the most frequently cited example of Western interference and of its consequences is the overthrow of the Mosaddeq government in Iran in 1953. The crisis began when the popular nationalist leader Mosaddeq decided, with general support in the country, to nationalize the oil companies, and in particular the most important of them, the Anglo-Iranian Company. Certainly, the terms under which this and other concessionary oil companies operated were rightly seen as both unequal and unfavorable. For example, the Anglo-Iranian oil company paid more in taxes to the British government than in royalties to the government of Iran. The United States became involved first as an ally of Britain and then, increasingly, through fear of Soviet involvement on the side of Mosaddeq's government. The American and British governments therefore decided, allegedly in agreement with the shah, to get rid of Mosaddeq by means of a coup d'état. At first, the coup did not go very well. Mosaddeq simply arrested the shah's messenger and ordered the arrest of General Zahedi, the leader of the coup and the intended head of the shah's new government. For a while Mosaddeq's supporters and members of the Tudeh Communist Party held mass demonstrations in the streets, denouncing both the shah and his father and crying, "Yankees go home." The shah himself fled with his wife to Iraq, where he met secretly with the U.S. ambassador, and then flew on to Rome.

Meanwhile the demonstrations in Tehran changed in character. Previously they had all been against the shah; now they began to favor him, and in particular the military appeared in the streets supporting the shah. After a series of demonstrations, Mosaddeq was overthrown and Zahedi replaced him as prime minister. On August 19, 1953, the news reached the shah in a telegram from AP: "Tehran: Mosaddeq overthrown. Imperial troops control Tehran. Zahedi Prime Minister." Soon after, the shah returned to Tehran and resumed his throne.

The aftermath, by the standards of the region, was remarkably mild. The foreign minister of Mosaddeq's government was executed and a number of his supporters sentenced to imprisonment. Mosaddeq himself was put on trial and sentenced to three years' house arrest. After his release in August 1956 he lived under guard on his estate until 1967. Because of the active intervention of the American CIA and the British MI6 in the overthrow of the regime and the return of the shah, the shah was regarded by significant groups of his subjects as at first a British, then an American puppet.

If so, the puppeteers were neither reliable nor efficient. When the Iranian Revolution came in 1979, neither the British nor the Americans did anything to save the shah from overthrow. The U.S. administration at the time not only provided no help but made it clear that they had no intention of doing anything. Even more dramatically, they for a while refused the shah and his family asylum in the United States. The shah fled Tehran in mid-January 1979 and flew via Egypt to Morocco, where he stayed briefly as a guest of the king. But the king of Morocco had other concerns, notably a meeting of the Organization of the Islamic Conference, which he was to host in Rabat in early April. King Hassan therefore asked the shah to leave not later than March 30. The shah informed the U.S. ambassador that he would now like to accept President Carter's offer of asylum, only to discover that that offer had been withdrawn, apparently in the belief that establishing good relations with the new rulers of Iran took precedence over granting asylum to the shah and his family. The United States relented only when the shah was dying and in acute need of medical care. On October 22, 1979, the shah was informed that he could proceed to the United States. He arrived in New York early the next morning and went straight to the hospital. Becoming aware that his presence was causing problems to the United States, in spite of his serious illness he left the country and went to Panama, where he narrowly escaped extradition to Iran, and from Panama he returned to Egypt, where he died in 1980.

Different groups in the region drew two lessons from these events—one, that the Americans were willing to use both force and intrigue to install or restore their puppet rulers in Middle Eastern countries; the other, that they were not reliable patrons when these puppets were seriously attacked by their own people, and would simply abandon them. The one evoked hatred, the other contempt—a dangerous combination.

Clearly, something deeper is involved than these specific grievances, numerous and important as they may be, something deeper which turns every disagreement into a problem and makes every problem insoluble. What we confront now is not just a complaint about one or another American policy but rather a rejection and condemnation, at once angry and contemptuous, of all that America is seen to represent in the modern world.

A key figure in the development of these new attitudes was Sayyid Qutb, an Egyptian who became a leading ideologue of Muslim fundamentalism and an active member of the fundamentalist organization known as the Muslim Brothers. Born in a village in Upper Egypt in 1906, he studied in Cairo and for some years worked as a teacher and then as an official in the Egyptian Ministry of Education. In that capacity he was sent on a special study mission to the United States, where he stayed from November 1948 to August 1950. His fundamentalist activism and writing began very soon after his return from America to Egypt. After the military coup of July 1952, he at first maintained close relations with the so-called Free Officers, but he parted company with them as his Islamist teachings clashed with their secularist policies. After several brushes with the authorities, he was sentenced, in 1955, to fifteen years' imprisonment. As a result of an intercession on his behalf by President Arif of Iraq, he was released in 1964, and he published one of his major works, *Ma'ālim fī'l-Tarīq* (*Signposts on the Way*), later that year. On August 9, 1965, he was arrested again, this time on charges of treason and, specifically, of planning the assassination of President Nasser. After a summary trial he was sentenced to death on August 21, 1966. The sentence was carried out eight days later.

Sayyid Qutb's stay in the United States seems to have been a crucial period in the development of his ideas concerning the relations between Islam and the outside world and, more particularly, within itself. The State of Israel had just been established and survived by fighting and winning the first of a series of Arab-Israel wars. This was a time when the world was becoming aware of the near total destruction of the Jews in Nazi-ruled Europe, and public opinion in America, as in much of the world, was overwhelmingly on the Israeli side. The wartime relationship between the Third Reich and prominent Arab leaders such as the Mufti of Jerusalem and Rashid 'Ali of Iraq was also in the news, and popular sympathy went naturally to those seen as Hitler's victims in their struggle to escape destruction by Hitler's accomplices. Sayyid Qutb was shocked by the level of support in America for what he saw as a Jewish onslaught on Islam, with Christian complicity.

Even more revealing was his shocked response to the

American way of life—principally its sinfulness and degeneracy and its addiction to what he saw as sexual promiscuity. Sayyid Qutb took as a given the contrast between Eastern spirituality and Western materialism, and described America as a particularly extreme form of the latter. Everything in America, he wrote, even religion, is measured in material terms. He observed that there were many churches but warned his readers that their number should not be misunderstood as an expression of real religious or spiritual feeling. Churches in America, he said, operate like businesses, competing for clients and for publicity, and using the same methods as stores and theaters to attract customers and audiences. For the minister of a church, as for the manager of a business or a theater, success is what matters, and success is measured by size—bigness, numbers. To attract clientele, churches advertise shamelessly and offer what Americans most seek—"a good time" or "fun" (he cited the English words in his Arabic text). The result is that church recreation halls, with the blessing of the priesthood, hold dances where people of both sexes meet, mix, and touch. The ministers even go so far as to dim the lights in order to facilitate the fury of the dance. "The dance is inflamed by the notes of the gramophone," he noted with evident disgust; "the dance-hall becomes a whirl of heels and thighs, arms enfold hips, lips and breasts meet, and the air is full of lust." He also quoted the Kinsey Reports on sexual behavior to document his description and condemnation of universal American debauchery.[4] This perception of the West and its ways may help explain why pious terrorists regard dance halls, nightclubs, and other places where young men and women meet as legitimate targets. So vehement were Sayyid Qutb's denunciations of the American way of life that in 1952 he was obliged to leave his post in the Ministry of Education. It was apparently after this that he joined the Muslim Brothers.

The main thrust of Sayyid Qutb's writing and preaching was directed against the internal enemy—what he called the new age of ignorance, in Arabic *jāhiliyya,* a classical Islamic term for the period of paganism that prevailed in Arabia before the advent of the Prophet and of Islam. As Sayyid Qutb saw it, a new *jāhiliyya* had engulfed the Muslim peoples and the new pharaohs—rightly seen as an allusion to the existing regimes—who were ruling them. But the threat of the external enemy was great and growing.

It has been suggested that Sayyid Qutb's anti-Americanism is the result simply of the fact that he happened to visit America, and that he would have reacted similarly had he been sent by his ministry to any European country. But by that time, America was what mattered, and its leadership, for good or evil, of the non-Islamic world was increasingly recognized and discussed. The sinfulness and also the degeneracy of America and its consequent threat to Islam and the Muslim peoples became articles of faith in Muslim fundamentalist circles.

By now there is an almost standardized litany of American offenses recited in the lands of Islam, in the media, in pamphlets, in sermons, and in public speeches. A notable example was in an address by an Egyptian professor at the joint meeting of the European Union and the Organization of the Islamic Conference held in Istanbul in February 2002. The crime sheet goes back to the original settlement

in North America, and what is described as the expropria-
tion and extermination of the previous inhabitants and the
sustained ill treatment of the survivors among them. It continues with the enslavement, importation, and exploitation
of the blacks (an odd accusation coming from that particular source) and of immigrants in the United States. It
includes war crimes against Japan at Hiroshima and
Nagasaki, as well as in Korea, Vietnam, Somalia, and elsewhere. Noteworthy among these crimes of imperialist
aggression are American actions in Lebanon, Khartoum,
Libya, Iraq, and of course helping Israel against the Palestinians. More broadly, the charge sheet includes support for
Middle Eastern and other tyrants, such as the shah of Iran
and Haile Selassie of Ethiopia, as well as a variable list of
Arab tyrants, adjusted to circumstances, against their own
peoples.

Yet the most powerful accusation of all is the degeneracy
and debauchery of the American way of life, and the threat
that it offers to Islam. This threat, classically formulated by
Sayyid Qutb, became a regular part of the vocabulary and
ideology of Islamic fundamentalists, and most notably, in
the language of the Iranian Revolution. This is what is
meant by the term the Great Satan, applied to the United
States by the late Ayatollah Khomeini. Satan as depicted in
the Qur'an is neither an imperialist nor an exploiter. He is a
seducer, "the insidious tempter who whispers in the hearts
of men" (Qur'an CXIV, 4, 5).

# V

## *Satan and the Soviets*

America's new role—and the Middle East's perception of it—was vividly illustrated by an incident in Pakistan in 1979. On November 20, a band of a thousand Muslim religious radicals seized the Great Mosque in Mecca and held it for a time against the Saudi security forces. Their declared aim was to "purify Islam" and liberate the holy land of Arabia from the "royal clique of infidels" and the corrupt religious leaders who supported them. Their leader, in speeches played from loudspeakers, denounced Westerners as the destroyers of fundamental Islamic values and the Saudi government as their accomplices. He called for a return to the old Islamic traditions of "justice and equality." After some hard fighting, the rebels were suppressed. Their leader was executed on January 9, 1980, along with sixty-two of his followers, among them Egyptians, Kuwaitis, Yemenis, and citizens of other Arab countries.

Meanwhile, a demonstration in support of the rebels took place in the Pakistani capital, Islamabad. A rumor had circulated—endorsed by Ayatollah Khomeini, who was then in the process of establishing himself as the revolutionary leader in Iran—that American troops had been involved in the clashes in Mecca. The American Embassy was attacked by a crowd of Muslim demonstrators, and two

Americans and two Pakistani employees were killed. Why had Khomeini stood by a report that was not only false but wildly improbable?

These events took place within the context of the Iranian Revolution of 1979. On November 4, the United States Embassy in Tehran was seized, and sixty-two Americans taken hostage. Ten of them, women and African Americans, were promptly released; the remaining hostages were then held for 444 days, until their release on January 20, 1981. The motives for this, baffling to many at the time, have become clearer since, thanks to subsequent statements and revelations from the hostage takers and others. It is now apparent that the hostage crisis occurred not because relations between Iran and the United States were deteriorating but because they were improving. In the fall of 1979, the relatively moderate Iranian prime minister, Mehdi Bazargan, had arranged to meet with the American national security adviser, Zbigniew Brzezinski, under the aegis of the Algerian government. The two men met on November 1 and were reported to have been photographed shaking hands. There seemed to be a real possibility—in the eyes of the radicals, a real danger—that there might be some accommodation between the two countries. Protesters seized the embassy and took the American diplomats hostage in order to destroy any hope of further dialogue. In this they were, for the time being at least, completely successful.

For Khomeini, the United States was the main enemy against whom he had to wage his holy war for Islam. Then, as in the past, this world of unbelievers was seen as the only serious force rivaling and preventing the divinely ordained spread and triumph of Islam. In Khomeini's earlier writing, and notably in his 1970 book *Islamic Government,* the United States is mentioned infrequently, and then principally in the context of imperialism—first as the helper, then as the successor of the more familiar British Empire. By the time of the revolution, and the direct confrontation to which it gave rise, the United States had become, for him, the principal adversary, and the central target for Muslim rage and contempt.

Khomeini's special hostility to the United States seems to date from October 1964, when he made a speech in front of his residence in Qum, passionately denouncing the law submitted to the Iranian Assembly giving extraterritorial status to the American military mission, together with their families, staffs, advisers, and servants, and immunity from Iranian jurisdiction. He was apparently not aware that similar immunities had been requested and granted, as a matter of course, to the American forces stationed in Britain during World War II. But the question of the so-called capitulations, extraterritorial immunities accorded in the past to Western merchants and other travelers in Islamic lands, was a sensitive one, and Khomeini played on it skillfully. "They have reduced the Iranian people to a level lower than that of an American dog. If someone runs over a dog belonging to an American, he will be prosecuted. Even if the Shah himself were to run over a dog belonging to an American, he would be prosecuted. But if an American cook runs over the Shah, the head of state, no one will have the right to interfere with him."[1] Already in trouble with the authorities, as a result of this speech Khomeini was exiled from Iran on November 4. He returned to this theme in a number of later speeches and writings, taunting the Americans in particular with their alleged commitment to human rights and their disregard of these rights in Iran and in other places, including Latin America, "in their own hemisphere." Other accusations include the looting of Iran's wealth and support of Iran's monarchy.

In speeches after his return to Iran, the list of grievances and the list of enemies both grew longer, but America now headed the list. And not only in Iran. In a speech delivered in September 1979 in Qum, he complained that the whole Islamic world was caught in America's clutches and called on the Muslims of the world to unite against their enemy. It was about this time that he began to speak of America as "the Great Satan." About this time too he denounced both Anwar Sadat of Egypt and Saddam Hussein of Iraq as servants and agents of America. Sadat served America by making peace with Israel; Saddam Hussein did America's work by making war on Iran. The confrontation with America in the hostage crisis, in the Iraqi invasion, and on many diplomatic and economic battlefields confirmed Khomeini's judgment of America's central position in the struggle between Islam and the West. From now on America was "the Great Satan," Israel, seen as America's agent, was "the Little Satan," and "death to America" the order of the day. This was the slogan brandished and shouted in the anti-American demonstrations of 1979. Later it was given a ceremonial, almost ritualized quality that drained it of most of its real meaning.

American observers, awakened by the rhetoric of the Iranian Revolution to their new status as the Great Satan, tried to find reasons for the anti-American sentiment that had been intensifying in the Islamic world for some time. One explanation, which was for a while widely accepted, particularly in American foreign policy circles, was that America's image had been tarnished by its wartime and continuing alliance with the former colonial powers of Europe. In their country's defense, some American commentators pointed out that, unlike the Western European imperialists, America had itself been a victim of colonialism; the United States was the first country to win freedom from British rule. But the hope that the Middle Eastern subjects of the former British and French Empires would accept the American Revolution as a model for their own anti-imperialist struggle rested on a basic fallacy that Arab writers were quick to point out. The American Revolution, as they frequently remark, was fought not by Native American nationalists but by British settlers, and far from being a victory against colonialism, it represented colonialism's ultimate triumph; the English in North America succeeded in colonizing the land so thoroughly that they no longer needed the support of the mother country against the original inhabitants.

It is hardly surprising that former colonial subjects in the Middle East would see America as being tainted by the same kind of imperialism as Western Europe. But Middle Eastern resentment of imperial powers has not always been consistent. The Soviet Union, which retained and extended the imperial conquests of the czars of Russia, ruled with no light hand over tens of millions of Muslim subjects in Central Asia and in the Caucasus. And yet the Soviet Union suffered no similar backlash of anger and hatred from the Arab community.

Russia's interest in the Middle East was not new. The czars had been expanding southward and eastward for centuries, and had incorporated vast Muslim territories in their empire, at the expense of Turkey and Persia and the formerly independent Muslim states of Central Asia. The defeat of the Axis in 1945 brought a new Soviet threat. The Soviets were now strongly entrenched in the Balkans and could threaten Turkey on both its eastern and its western frontiers. They were already inside Iran, in occupation of the Persian province of Azerbaijan. Their threat to Iran was of long standing. In the Russo-Iranian wars of 1804–1813 and 1826–1828, the Russians had acquired the northern part of Azerbaijan, which became a province of the czarist empire and later a republic of the Soviet Union. In World War II, together with the British, the Soviets occupied Iran, to secure its lines of communication for their mutual use. When the war ended the British withdrew; the Soviets stayed, apparently with the intention of adding what remained of Azerbaijan to the Soviet Union.

That time they were held back. Thanks largely to American support, the Turks were able to refuse the Soviet demand for bases in the Straits, while the Iranians dismantled the Communist puppet state which the Soviet occupiers had set up in Persian Azerbaijan and reasserted the sovereignty of the government of Iran over all its territories.

For a while, the Soviet attempt to realize the age-old dream of the czars was resisted, and both Turkey and Iran entered into Western alliances. But the Russian-Egyptian arms agreement of 1955 brought Russia back into the Middle Eastern game, this time with a leading role. The

Turks and Iranians had long experience of Russian imperialism and were correspondingly wary. The Arab states' experience of imperialism was exclusively Western, and they were disposed to look more favorably on the Soviets. By leapfrogging the northern barrier and dealing directly with the newly independent Arab states, the Russians were able, within a short time, to establish a very strong position.

At first they proceeded in much the same way as their Western European predecessors—military bases, supply of weapons, military "guidance," economic and cultural penetration. But for Soviet-style relationships this was only a beginning, and the intention clearly was to carry it much further. There can be little doubt that, had it not been for American opposition, the Cold War, and the eventual collapse of the Soviet Union, the Arab world would at best have shared the fate of Poland and Hungary, more probably that of Uzbekistan. And that is not all. While seeking to establish a protectorate over their Middle Eastern allies, the Soviets showed themselves to be very ineffectual protectors. In the Arab-Israel War of 1967 and again in 1973, they were unwilling or unable to save their protégés from defeat and humiliation. The best they could do was to join with the United States in calling a halt to the Israeli advance.

By the early 1970s the Soviet presence was becoming not only ineffectual but also irksome. Like their Western imperial predecessors, the Soviets had established military bases on Egyptian soil which no Egyptian could enter and proceeded to the classic next stage of unequal treaties.

There were some Middle Eastern leaders who learned the lesson and turned, with greater or lesser reluctance, toward the West. Notable among them was President Anwar Sadat of Egypt, who had inherited the Soviet relationship from his predecessor, President Nasser. In May 1971 he was induced to sign a very unequal "Treaty of Friendship and Cooperation" with the USSR;[2] in July 1972 he ordered his Soviet military advisers to leave the country and took the first steps toward a rapprochement with the United States and a peace with Israel. President Sadat however seems to have been almost alone in his assessment and his policies, and in general these events seem to have brought no diminution in goodwill to the Soviets, and no corresponding increase in goodwill to the United States. The Soviets suffered no penalties or even reproof for their suppression of Islam in the Central Asian and Transcaucasian republics, where two hundred mosques were licensed to serve the religious needs of 50 million Muslims. Nor for that matter were the Chinese condemned for their battles against Muslims in Sinkiang. Nor did the Americans receive any credit for their efforts to save Muslims in Bosnia, Kosovo, and Albania. Obviously, other considerations were at work.

Perhaps the most dramatic illustration of this disparity was the Soviet invasion of Afghanistan in late December 1979 and the installation there of a puppet government. It would be difficult to find a clearer and more obvious case of imperialist aggression, conquest, and domination. And yet the response from the Arab and more generally the Islamic world was remarkably muted. By January 14, 1980, after long delays, the United Nations General Assembly was at last able to pass a resolution on this event, not as had been suggested, condemning Soviet aggression but "strongly deploring the recent armed intervention in Afghanistan." The word *aggression* was not used, and the "intervener" was not named. The vote was carried by 104 to 18. Among the Arab countries, Syria and Algeria abstained; South Yemen voted against the resolution; Libya was absent. The nonvoting PLO observer made a speech strongly defending the Soviet action. The Organization of the Islamic Conference did not do much better. On January 27, after much maneuvering and negotiation, the OIC managed to hold a meeting in Islamabad and to discuss the Soviet-Afghan issue. Two member states, South Yemen and Syria, boycotted the meeting; Libya's delegate delivered a violent attack on the USA, while the representative of the PLO, a full member of the OIC, abstained from voting on the anti-Soviet resolution and submitted his reservations in writing.

There was some response in the Muslim world to the Soviet invasion—some Saudi money, some Egyptian weapons, and many Arab volunteers. But it was left to the United States to organize, with some success, an Islamic counterattack to Soviet imperialism in Afghanistan. The OIC did little to help the Afghans, preferring to concentrate its attention on other matters—some small Muslim populations in areas not yet decolonized, and of course the Israel-Palestine conflict.

Israel is one among many points—Nigeria, Sudan, Bosnia, Kosovo, Macedonia, Chechnya, Sinkiang, Kashmir, Timor, Mindanao, et cetera—where the Islamic and non-Islamic worlds meet. Each of these is the central issue for those involved in it, and an annoying digression for the others. Westerners by contrast tend to give the greatest importance to those grievances which they hope can be satisfied at someone else's expense. The Israel-Palestine conflict has certainly attracted far more attention than any of the others, for several reasons. First, since Israel is a democracy and an open society, it is much easier to report—and misreport—what is going on there. Second, Jews are involved, and this can usually ensure a significant audience among those who for one reason or another are for or against them. A good example of this difference is the Iraq-Iran war, which was waged for eight years from 1980 to 1988. It caused vastly more death and destruction than all the Arab-Israel wars put together, but received far less attention. For one thing, neither Iraq nor Iran is a democracy, and reporting was therefore more difficult and more hazardous. For another, Jews were not involved, neither as victims nor as perpetrators, and reporting was therefore less interesting.

A third and ultimately the most important reason for the primacy of the Palestine issue is that it is, so to speak, the licensed grievance—the only one that can be freely and safely expressed in those Muslim countries where the media are either wholly owned or strictly overseen by the government. Indeed, Israel serves as a useful stand-in for complaints about the economic privation and political repression under which most Muslim peoples live, and as a way of deflecting the resulting anger. This method is vastly helped by the Israeli domestic scene, where any misdeed of the government, the army, the settlers, or anyone else is at once revealed and any falsehood at once exposed by Israeli critics, both Jews and Arabs, in the Israeli media and parliament. Most of Israel's antagonists suffer from no such impediment in their public diplomacy.

As the Western European empires faded, Middle Eastern anti-Americanism was attributed to other, more specific causes: economic exploitation, often described as the pillaging of the Islamic lands' resources; the support of corrupt local tyrants who serve America's purposes by oppressing and robbing their own people, and more and more, another cause: American support for Israel, first in its conflict with the Palestinian Arabs, then in its conflict with the neighboring Arab states and the larger Islamic world. There is certainly support for this hypothesis in Arab and Persian statements, but the argument that without one or another of these impediments all would have been well for American policies in the Middle East seems a little implausible. The Palestine problem has certainly caused great and growing anger, from time to time renewed and aggravated by policies and actions of Israeli governments or parties. But can it really be, as some contend, the prime cause of anti-Western sentiment?

Certain incongruities appear and recur in the historical record. In the 1930s, Nazi Germany's policies were the main cause of Jewish migration to Palestine, then a British mandate, and the consequent reinforcement of the Jewish community there. The Nazis not only permitted this migration; they facilitated it until the outbreak of the war, while the British, in the somewhat forlorn hope of winning Arab goodwill, imposed and enforced restrictions. Nevertheless, the Palestinian leadership of the time, and many other Arab leaders, supported the Germans, who sent the Jews to Palestine, rather than the British, who tried to keep them out.

The same kind of discrepancy can be seen in the events leading to and following the establishment of the State of Israel, in 1948. The Soviet Union played a significant role in procuring the majority by which the General Assembly of the United Nations voted to establish a Jewish state in Palestine and then gave Israel immediate *de jure* recognition. The United States was more hesitant and gave only *de facto* recognition. More important, the American government maintained a partial arms embargo on Israel, while Czechoslovakia, with Moscow's authorization, immediately sent a supply of weaponry which enabled the new state to survive. The reason for this Soviet policy at the time was neither goodwill toward the Jews nor ill will toward the Arabs. It was based on the mistaken—but at that time widely shared—belief that Britain was still the main power of the West and therefore Moscow's principal rival. On this basis, anyone making trouble for the British—as the Jews had done in the last years of the Palestine Mandate—was deserving of Soviet support. Later, Stalin realized his error and devoted his attention to America rather than Britain.

In the decade that followed the founding of Israel, American dealings with the Jewish state continued to be limited and cautious. After the Suez War of 1956, the United States intervened, forcefully and decisively, to secure the withdrawal of the Israeli, British, and French forces. The Soviet leader Khrushchev, who had remained cautiously silent in the earlier stages of the war, realized that a pro-Arab statement brought no danger of a collision with the United States and then—and only then—came out strongly on the Arab side. As late as the war of 1967, Israel relied for its weaponry on European, mainly French suppliers, not on the United States.

Nevertheless, the return of Russian imperialism, now in the form of the Soviet Union, to a more active role in Middle Eastern affairs brought an enthusiastic response in the Arab world. After some diplomatic visits and other activities, the new relationship came into the open with the official announcement, at the end of September 1955, of an arms deal signed between the Soviet Union and Egypt, which during the following years became more and more a Soviet satellite. More dramatic even than the arms deal itself was its welcome in the Arab world, transcending local differences and grievances. The Chambers of Deputies in Syria, Lebanon, and Jordan met immediately and voted resolutions of congratulation to then Prime Minister Nasser; even Nuri Said, the pro-Western ruler of Iraq and Nasser's rival for pan-Arab leadership, felt obliged to congratulate his Egyptian colleague. Almost the entire Arabic press gave its enthusiastic approval.

Why this response? Certainly the Arabs had no special love of Russia, nor did Muslims in the Arab world or elsewhere desire to bring either Communist ideology or Soviet power to their lands. Nor was it a reward for Moscow's Israel policy, which had been rather friendly. What delighted the Arabs was that they saw the arms deal—no doubt correctly—as a slap in the face for the West. The slap, and the visibly disconcerted Western and more particularly American response, reinforced the mood of hate and spite toward the West and encouraged its exponents.

The spread of Soviet influence in the Middle East and the enthusiastic response to it encouraged the United States to look more favorably on Israel, now seen as a reliable and potentially useful ally in a largely hostile region. Today, it is often forgotten that the strategic relationship between the United States and Israel was a consequence, not a cause, of Soviet penetration.

The first concern of any American government is of course to define U.S. interests and to devise policies for their protection and advancement. In the period following the Second World War, American policy in the Middle East, as elsewhere, was dominated by the need to prevent Soviet penetration. The United States regretfully relinquished the moral superiority of the sidelines and became involved in stages: first supporting the crumbling British position and, then, when that clearly became untenable, intervening more directly and, finally, replacing Britain as defender of the Middle East against outside attack, specifically from the Soviet Union.

The immediate postwar need was to resist Soviet pressure on the northern tier—to secure the Soviet withdrawal from Iranian Azerbaijan and to counter demands on Turkey. This policy was clear and intelligible and, on the whole, successful in saving Turkey and Iran. But the attempt to extend it to the Arab world by means of the Baghdad Pact backfired disastrously and antagonized or undermined those it was intended to attract. The Egyptian leader, Gamal 'Abd al-Nasser, seeing the pact as a threat to his leadership, turned to the Soviets; the pro-Western regime in Iraq was overthrown, and friendly regimes in Jordan and Lebanon were endangered to the point that both needed Western military help in order to survive. From 1955, when the Soviets leapfrogged across the northern tier into the Arab world, both the threat and the means of countering it changed radically. While the northern tier held firm, the Arab lands became hostile or, at best, nervously neutral. In this situation the American relationship with Israel entered a new phase.

This relationship was for a long time shaped by two entirely different considerations: one of which one might call ideological or sentimental; the other one, strategic. Americans, schooled on the Bible and on their own history, can readily see the birth of modern Israel as a new Exodus and a return to the Promised Land, and find it easy to empathize with people who seem to be repeating the experience of the pilgrim fathers, the pioneers, and their successors. The Arabs, of course, do not see it that way, and many Europeans share their view.

The other bond between the United States and Israel is the strategic relationship, which began in the 1960s, flourished in the 1970s and 1980s, fluctuated in the 1990s, and acquired a new importance when the United States faced the concurrent threats of Saddam Hussein's hegemonic ambitions, of al-Qa'ida's fundamentalist terror, and of deep-rooted and growing discontents among America's Arab allies. The value of Israel to the United States as a strategic asset has been much disputed. There have been some in the United States who view Israel as a major strategic ally in the region and the one sure bastion against both external and regional enemies. Others have argued that Israel, far from being a strategic asset, has been a strategic liability, by embittering U.S. relations with the Arab world and causing the failure of U.S. policies in the region.

But if one compares the record of American policy in the Middle East with that of other regions, one is struck not by its failure but by its success. There is, after all, no Vietnam in the Middle East, no Cuba or Nicaragua or El Salvador, not even an Angola. On the contrary, throughout the successive crises that have shaken the region, there has always been an imposing political, economic, and cultural American presence, usually in several countries—and this, until the Gulf War of 1991, without the need for any significant military intervention. And even then, their presence was needed to rescue the victims of an inter-Arab aggression, unrelated to either Israelis or Palestinians. Those who look only at the Middle East are constantly aware of the difficulties and failures of policy in that region, but if one looks at the picture in a wider perspective, one cannot but be astonished at the effectiveness of American policy in the Middle East as contrasted with, say, Southeast Asia, Central America, or southern Africa.

Since the collapse of the Soviet Union, a new American policy has emerged in the Middle East, concerned with different objectives. Its main aim is to prevent the emergence of a regional hegemony—of a single regional power that could dominate the area and thus establish monopolistic control of Middle Eastern oil. This has been the basic concern underlying successive American policies toward Iran, Iraq, or to any other perceived future threat within the region.

The policy adopted so far, in order to prevent such a hegemony, is to encourage, arm, and when necessary support a regional and therefore mainly Arab security pact. This policy inevitably evokes the unhappy memory of earlier attempts, which did more harm than good. This time the proposed pact may have a somewhat better chance. The presumed enemy is no longer the redoubtable

Soviet Union, and regional rulers are taking a more sober view of the world and their place in it. But such a pact, based on unstable regimes ruling volatile societies, is inherently precarious, and the chain is no stronger than its weakest link. The recent history of Iraq illustrates the different ways that such a policy can go wrong. By embracing the Shah, the U.S. procured his overthrow; by fostering Saddam Hussein, it nurtured a monster. It would be fatally easy to repeat either or both of these errors, with considerable risk to Western interests in the region and terrible consequences for the people who live there.

In this context the willingness of some Arab governments to negotiate peace with Israel, and the American concern to push the peace process along become intelligible. Many Arabs began to realize that on the best estimate of Israel's strength and the worst estimate of Israel's intentions Israel is not their most serious problem, nor is it the greatest threat that confronts them. An Israel at war with its neighbors would be a constant danger, a distraction that could always be used by a new—or even the same—Saddam Hussein. But an Israel at peace with its neighbors could provide, at the very least, an element of democratic stability in the region.

There are, in general, two quite different kinds of alliance. One of them is strategic and may be a purely temporary accommodation on the basis of perceived common threats. Such an accommodation may be reached with any type of ruler—the kind of government he runs, the kind of society he governs are equally irrelevant. The other party to such an alliance can change his mind at any time, or may have it changed for him if he is overthrown and replaced.

The alliance may thus be ended by a change of regime, a change of leader, or even a change in outlook. What can happen is well illustrated by events in Libya, Iraq, Iran, and the Sudan, where political changes brought total reversals of policy, or in another sense by Egypt, where even without a change of regime rulers were able to switch from the West to the Soviets and back again to a Western alignment.

The same flexibility also exists on the American side. Just as such allies can at any time abandon the United States, the United States has obviously also felt free to abandon such allies, if the alliance becomes too troublesome or ceases to be cost-effective—as, for example, in South Vietnam, Kurdistan, and Lebanon. In abandoning an ally with which there is no more than a strategic accommodation, one can proceed without compunction and without risk of serious criticism at home.

The other kind of alliance is one based on a genuine affinity of institutions, aspirations, and way of life—and is far less subject to change. The Soviets in their heyday were well aware of this and tried to create communist dictatorships wherever they went. Democracies are more difficult to create. They are also more difficult to destroy.

# VI

# Double Standards

Increasingly in recent decades, Middle Easterners have articulated a more sensitive complaint, a new grievance against American policy: not just American complicity with imperialism or with Zionism but something nearer home and more immediate—American complicity with the corrupt tyrants who rule over them. For obvious reasons, this particular complaint does not often appear in public discourse, nor is it likely to be mentioned in conversations between foreign ministry officials and diplomats. Middle Eastern governments, such as those of Iraq, Syria, and the Palestine Authority, have developed great skill in controlling their own media and manipulating those of Western countries. Nor, for equally obvious reasons, is it raised in diplomatic negotiation. But it is discussed, with increasing anguish and urgency, in private conversations with listeners who can be trusted, and recently even in public—and not only by Islamic radicals, for whom it is a, indeed the, major issue. Interestingly, the Iranian Revolution of 1979 was one time when this resentment was expressed openly. The shah was accused of supporting America, but America was also attacked for imposing what the revolutionaries saw as an impious and tyrannical leader as its puppet. In the years that followed, Iranians discovered that pious tyrants could be as bad as impious tyrants or worse, and that this brand of tyranny could not be blamed on foreign sponsors or models.

There is some justice in one charge that is frequently leveled against the United States, and more generally against the West: Middle Easterners increasingly complain that the West judges them by different and lower standards than it does Europeans and Americans, both in what is expected of them and in what they may expect, in terms of their economic well-being and their political freedom. They assert that Western spokesmen repeatedly overlook or even defend actions and support rulers that they would not tolerate in their own countries.

Relatively few in the Western world nowadays think of themselves as engaged in a confrontation with Islam. But there is nevertheless a widespread perception that there are significant differences between the advanced Western world and the rest, notably the peoples of Islam, and that these latter are in some ways different, with the usually tacit assumption that they are inferior. The most flagrant violations of civil rights, political freedom, even human decency are disregarded or glossed over, and crimes against humanity, which in a European or American country would evoke a storm of outrage, are seen as normal and even acceptable. Regimes that practice such violations are not only tolerated, but even elected to the Human Rights Commission of the United Nations, whose members include Saudi Arabia, Syria, Sudan, and Libya.

The underlying assumption in all this is that these peoples are incapable of running a democratic society and have neither concern nor capacity for human decency. They will in any case be governed by corrupt despotisms. It is not the West's business to correct them, still less to change them, but merely to ensure that the despots are friendly rather than hostile to Western interests. In this perspective it is dangerous to tamper with the existing order, and those who seek better lives for themselves and their countrymen are disparaged, often actively discouraged. It is simpler, cheaper, and safer to replace a troublesome tyrant with an amenable tyrant, rather than face the unpredictable hazards of regime change, especially of a change brought about by the will of the people expressed in a free election.

The "devil-you-know" principle seems to underlie the foreign policies of many Western governments toward the peoples of the Islamic world. This attitude is sometimes presented and even accepted as an expression of sympathy and support for the Arabs and their causes, apparently in the belief that by exempting Arab rulers and leaders from the normal rules of civilized behavior we are somehow conferring a boon on the Arab peoples. In fact this exemption is nothing of the kind, being at the very best a quest for a temporary alliance based on a shared self-interest and directed against a common enemy, sometimes also sustained by a shared prejudice. At a more profound level of reality, it is an expression of disrespect and unconcern—disrespect for the Arab past, unconcern for the Arab present and future.

This approach commands some support in both diplomatic and academic circles in the United States and rather more widely in Europe. Arab rulers are thus able to slaughter tens of thousands of their people, as in Syria and Algeria, or hundreds of thousands, as in Iraq and Sudan, to deprive men of most and women of all civil rights, and to indoctrinate children in their schools with bigotry and hatred against others, without incurring any significant protest from liberal media and institutions in the West, still less any hint of punishments such as boycotts, divestment, or indictment in Brussels. This so-to-speak diplomatic attitude toward Arab governments has in reality been profoundly harmful to the Arab peoples, a fact of which they are becoming painfully aware.

As many Middle Easterners see it, the European and American governments' basic position is: "We don't care what you do to your own people at home, so long as you are cooperative in meeting our needs and protecting our interests."

Sometimes, even where American interests are concerned, American governments have betrayed those whom they had promised to support and persuaded to take risks. A notable example occurred in 1991, when the United States called on the Iraqi people to revolt against Saddam Hussein. The Kurds in northern Iraq and the Shi'a in southern Iraq did so, and the victorious United States forces sat and watched while Saddam Hussein, using the helicopters that the cease-fire agreement had allowed him to retain, bloodily suppressed and slaughtered them, group by group and region by region.

The reasoning behind this action—or rather inaction—is not difficult to see. No doubt, the victorious Gulf War coalition wanted a change of government in Iraq, but they had hoped for a coup d'état, not a revolution. They saw a genuine popular uprising as dangerous—it could lead to uncertainty or even anarchy in the region. It might even produce a democratic state, an alarming prospect for America's "allies" in the region. A coup would be more predictable and could achieve the desired result: the replacement of Saddam Hussein by another, more cooperative dictator, who could take his place among those allies in the coalition. This policy failed miserably, and was variously interpreted in the region as treachery or weakness, foolishness or hypocrisy.

Another example of this double standard occurred in the Syrian city of Hama in 1982. The troubles in Hama began with an uprising headed by the radical Muslim Brothers. The Syrian government responded swiftly, and in force. They did not use water cannon and rubber bullets, nor did they send their soldiers to face snipers and booby traps in house-to-house searches to find and identify their enemies among the local, civil population. Their method was simpler, safer, and more expeditious. They attacked the city with tanks, artillery, and bomber aircraft, and followed these with bulldozers to complete the work of destruction. Within a very short time they had reduced a large part of the city to rubble. The number killed was estimated, by Amnesty International, at somewhere between ten thousand and twenty-five thousand.

The action, which was ordered and supervised by the Syrian president, Hafiz al-Assad, attracted little attention at the time. This meager response was in marked contrast with that evoked by another massacre, a few months later in the same year, in the Palestinian refugee camps in Sabra and Shatila, in Lebanon. On that occasion, some seven or eight hundred Palestinians were massacred by a Lebanese Christian militia allied to Israel. This evoked powerful and widespread condemnation of Israel, which has reverberated to the present day. The massacre in Hama did not prevent the United States from subsequently courting Assad, who received a long succession of visits from American Secretaries of State James Baker (eleven times between September 1990 and July 1992), Warren Christopher (fifteen times between February 1993 and February 1996), and Madeline Albright (four times between September 1997 and January 2000), and even from President Clinton (one visit to Syria and two meetings in Switzerland between January 1994 and March 2000). It is hardly likely that Americans would have been so eager to propitiate a ruler who had perpetrated such crimes on Western soil, with Western victims. Hafiz al-Assad never became an American ally or, as others would put it, puppet, but it was certainly not for lack of trying on the part of American diplomacy.

Fundamentalists were conscious of a different disparity—another no less dramatic case of double standards. Those whose slaughter in Hama aroused so little concern in the West were Muslim Brothers and their families and neighbors. In Western eyes, so it appeared, human rights did not apply to pious Muslim victims, nor democratic constraints to their "secular" murderers.

Western mistrust of Islamic political movements, and willingness to tolerate or even support dictators who kept such movements out of power appeared even more dramatically in the case of Algeria, where a new democratic constitution was adopted by referendum in February 1989 and the multiparty system officially established in July of that year. In December 1991, the Islamic Salvation Front (FIS) did very well in the first round of the elections for the

National Assembly and seemed more than likely to win a clear majority in the second round. The FIS had already challenged the Algerian military, accusing them of being more adept at repressing their own people than at helping a brother in need. The brother in need was Saddam Hussein, whose invasion of Kuwait and defiance of the West aroused great enthusiasm among Muslim fundamentalists in North Africa, and persuaded their leaders to transfer their allegiance from their Saudi sponsors to their new Iraqi hero. In January 1992, after an interval of growing tension, the military canceled the second round of elections. In the months that followed they dissolved the FIS and established a "secular" regime, in fact a ruthless dictatorship, with nods of approval in Paris, Washington, and other Western capitals. A bitter and murderous struggle followed, with reciprocal accusations of massacre—of fundamentalists by the army and other less formal instruments of the government, of secularists and modernists and uninvolved bystanders by the fundamentalists. In 1997 Amnesty International assessed the number of victims since the beginning of the struggle at eighty thousand, most of them civilians.

Al-Qa'ida has held the United States explicitly responsible for the military takeover in Algeria. Here as elsewhere America, as the dominant power in the world of the infidels, was naturally blamed for all that went wrong, and more specifically for the suppression of Islamist movements, the slaughter of their followers, and the establishment of what were seen as anti-Islamist dictatorships with Western—more specifically, American—support. Here too the Americans were blamed—by many for not protesting this violation of democratic liberties, by some for actively encouraging and supporting the military regime. Similar problems arise in Egypt, in Pakistan, and in some other Muslim countries where it seems likely that a genuinely free and fair election would result in an Islamist victory.

In this, the democrats are of course at a disadvantage. Their ideology requires them, even when in power, to give freedom and rights to the Islamist opposition. The Islamists, when in power, are under no such obligation. On the contrary, their principles require them to suppress what they see as impious and subversive activities.

For Islamists, democracy, expressing the will of the people, is the road to power, but it is a one-way road, on which there is no return, no rejection of the sovereignty of God, as exercised through His chosen representatives. Their electoral policy has been classically summarized as "One man (men only), one vote, once."

Clearly, in the Islamic world as it was in Europe, a free and fair election is the culmination, not the inauguration, of the process of democratic development. But that is no reason to cosset dictators.

# VII

## *A Failure of Modernity*

Almost the entire Muslim world is affected by poverty and tyranny. Both of these problems are attributed, especially by those with an interest in diverting attention from themselves, to America—the first to American economic dominance and exploitation, now thinly disguised as "globalization"; the second to America's support for the many so-called Muslim tyrants who serve its purposes. Globalization has become a major theme in the Arab media, and it is almost always raised in connection with American economic penetration. The increasingly wretched economic situation in most of the Muslim world, compared not only with the West but also with the rapidly rising economies of East Asia, fuels these frustrations. American paramountcy, as Middle Easterners see it, indicates where to direct the blame and the resulting hostility.

The combination of low productivity and high birth rate in the Middle East makes for an unstable mix, with a large and rapidly growing population of unemployed, uneducated, and frustrated young men. By all indicators from the United Nations, the World Bank, and other authorities, the Arab countries—in matters such as job creation, education, technology, and productivity—lag ever further behind the West. Even worse, the Arab nations also lag behind the more recent recruits to Western-style modernity, such as Korea, Taiwan, and Singapore.

The comparative figures on the performance of Muslim countries, as reflected in these statistics, are devastating. In the listing of economies by gross domestic product, the highest ranking Muslim majority country is Turkey, with 64 million inhabitants, in twenty-third place, between Austria and Denmark, with about 5 million each. The next is Indonesia, with 212 million, in twenty-eighth place, following Norway with 4.5 million and followed by Saudi Arabia with 21 million. In comparative purchasing power, the first Muslim state is Indonesia in fifteenth place, followed by Turkey in nineteenth place. The highest-ranking Arab country is Saudi Arabia, in twenty-ninth place, followed by Egypt. In living standards as reflected by gross domestic product per head, the first Muslim state is Qatar, in twenty-third place, followed by the United Arab Emirates in twenty-fifth place and Kuwait in twenty-eighth.

In a listing by industrial output, the highest-ranking Muslim country is Saudi Arabia, number twenty-one, followed by Indonesia, tied with Austria and Belgium in twenty-second place, and Turkey, tied with Norway in twenty-seventh place. In a listing by manufacturing output, the highest-ranking Arab country is Egypt, in thirty-fifth place, tying with Norway. In a listing by life expectancy, the first Arab state is Kuwait, in thirty-second place, following Denmark and followed by Cuba. In ownership of telephone lines per hundred people, the first Muslim country listed is the United Arab Emirates, in thirty-third place, following Macau and followed by Réunion. In ownership of computers per hundred people, the first Muslim state listed is

Bahrain, in thirtieth place, followed by Qatar in thirty-second and the United Arab Emirates in thirty-fourth.

Book sales present an even more dismal picture. A listing of twenty-seven countries, beginning with the United States and ending with Vietnam, does not include a single Muslim state. In a human development index, Brunei is number 32, Kuwait 36, Bahrain 40, Qatar 41, the United Arab Emirates 44, Libya 66, Kazakhstan 67, and Saudi Arabia tied with Brazil as number 68.

A report on Arab Human Development in 2002, prepared by a committee of Arab intellectuals and published under the auspices of the United Nations, again reveals some striking contrasts. "The Arab world translates about 330 books annually, one-fifth of the number that Greece translates. The accumulative total of translated books since the Caliph Maa'moun's [sic] time [the ninth century] is about 100,000, almost the average that Spain translates in one year." The economic situation is no better: "The GDP in all Arab countries combined stood at $531.2 billion in 1999—less than that of a single European country, Spain ($595.5 billion)." Another aspect of underdevelopment is illustrated in a table of "active research scientists, frequently cited articles, and frequently cited papers per million inhabitants, 1987."[1]

| Country | Research Scientists | Articles with 40 or more Citations | Number of Frequently Cited Papers per Million People |
|---|---|---|---|
| United States | 466,211 | 10,481 | 42.99 |
| India | 29,509 | 31 | 0.04 |
| Australia | 24,963 | 280 | 17.23 |
| Switzerland | 17,028 | 523 | 79.90 |
| China | 15,558 | 31 | 0.03 |
| Israel | 11,617 | 169 | 36.63 |
| Egypt | 3,782 | 1 | 0.02 |
| Republic of Korea | 2,255 | 5 | 0.12 |
| Saudi Arabia | 1,915 | 1 | 0.07 |
| Kuwait | 884 | 1 | 0.53 |
| Algeria | 362 | 1 | 0.01 |

This is hardly surprising, given the comparative figures for illiteracy.

In a ranking of 155 countries for economic freedom in 2001, the Arab Gulf states do rather well, with Bahrain number 9, the United Arab Emirates 14, and Kuwait 42. But the general economic performance of the Arab and more broadly the Muslim world remains relatively poor. According to the World Bank, in 2000 the average annual income in the Muslim countries from Morocco to Bangladesh was only half the world average, and in the 1990s the combined gross national products of Jordan, Syria, and Lebanon—that is, three of Israel's Arab neighbors—were considerably smaller than that of Israel alone.

The per capita figures are worse. According to United Nations statistics, Israel's per capita GDP was three and a half times that of Lebanon and Syria, twelve times that of Jordan, and thirteen and a half times that of Egypt.

The contrast with the West, and now also with the Far East, is even more disconcerting. In earlier times such discrepancies might have passed unnoticed by the vast mass of the population. Today, thanks to modern media and communications, even the poorest and most ignorant are painfully aware of the differences between themselves and others, alike at the personal, familial, local, and societal levels.

Modernization in politics has fared no better—perhaps even worse—than in warfare and economics. Many Islamic countries have experimented with democratic institutions of one kind or another. In some, as in Turkey and Iran, they were introduced by innovative native reformers; in others, as in several of the Arab countries, they were installed and then bequeathed by departing imperialists. The record, with the exception of Turkey, is one of almost unrelieved failure. Western-style parties and parliaments almost invariably ended in corrupt tyrannies, maintained by repression and indoctrination. The only European model that worked, in the sense of accomplishing its purposes, was the one-party dictatorship. The Ba'th Party, different branches of which have ruled Iraq and Syria for decades, incorporated the worst features of its Nazi and Soviet models. Since the death of the Egyptian president Nasser, in 1970, no Arab leader has been able to gain extensive support outside his own country. Indeed, no Arab leader has been willing to submit his claim to power to a free vote. The leaders who have come closest to winning pan-Arab approval are the Libyan Muʿammar Qaddafi in the 1970s and, more recently, Saddam Hussein. That these two, of all Arab rulers, should enjoy such wide popularity is in itself both appalling and revealing.

In view of this, it is hardly surprising that many Muslims speak of the failure of modernization and respond to different diagnoses of the sickness of their society, with different prescriptions for its cure.

For some, the answer is more and better modernization, bringing the Middle East into line with the modern and modernizing world. For others, modernity is itself the problem, and the source of all their woes.

The people of the Middle East are increasingly aware of the deep and widening gulf between the opportunities of the free world outside their borders and the appalling privation and repression within them. The resulting anger is naturally directed first against their rulers, and then against those whom they see as keeping those rulers in power for selfish reasons. It is surely significant that all the terrorists who have been identified in the September 11 attacks on New York and Washington came from Saudi Arabia and Egypt—that is, countries whose rulers are deemed friendly to the United States.

One reason for this curious fact, advanced by an Al-Qaʿida operative, is that terrorists from friendly countries have less trouble getting U.S. visas. A more basic reason is the deeper hostility in countries where the United States is held responsible for maintaining tyrannical regimes. A special case, now under increasing scrutiny, is Saudi Arabia, where significant elements in the regime itself seem at times to share and foster this hostility.

# VIII

## The Marriage of Saudi Power and Wahhabi Teaching

The rejection of modernity in favor of a return to the sacred past has a varied and ramified history in the region and has given rise to a number of movements. The most important of these was undoubtedly that known, after its founder, as Wahhabism. Muhammad ibn 'Abd al-Wahhab (1703–1792) was a theologian from the Najd area of Arabia, ruled by local sheikhs of the House of Saud. In 1744 he launched a campaign of purification and renewal. His declared aim was to return to the pure and authentic Islam of the Founder, removing and where necessary destroying all the later accretions and distortions.

The Wahhabi cause was embraced by the Saudi rulers of Najd, who promoted it, for a while successfully, by force of arms. In a series of campaigns, they carried their rule and their faith to much of central and eastern Arabia and even raided the lands of the Fertile Crescent under direct Ottoman administration. After sacking Karbala, the Shi'ite holy place in Iraq, they turned their attention to the Hijaz, and in 1804–1806 occupied and—in their terms—cleansed the holy cities of Mecca and Medina. By now they were clearly confronting and challenging the Ottoman sultan, whom the Saudi ruler denounced as a backslider from the

Muslim faith and a usurper in the Muslim state.

The Ottoman Empire, even at this stage of its decline, was able to cope with a desert rebel. With the help of the pasha of Egypt and his forces, the task was completed in 1818, when the Saudi capital was occupied and the Saudi emir sent to Istanbul and decapitated. For the time being, the Saudi state ceased to exist, but the Wahhabi doctrine survived, and from about 1823 another member of the House of Saud was able to reconstitute the Saudi principality, with its capital in Riyadh. Once again, the chieftains of the House of Saud helped and were helped by the exponents of Wahhabi doctrine.

The rise of Wahhabism in eighteenth-century Arabia was in significant measure a response to the changing circumstances of the time. One of these was of course the retreat of Islam and the corresponding advance of Christendom. This had been going on for a long time, but it was a slow and gradual process, and began at the remote peripheries of the Islamic world. By the eighteenth century it was becoming clear even at the center. The long, slow retreat of the Ottomans in the Balkans and the advance of the British in India were still far away from Arabia, but their impact was felt, both through the Ottomans on the one side and in the Persian Gulf on the other, and was surely reflected among the pilgrims who came to Arabia every year from all over the Muslim world. The ire of the Wahhabis was directed not primarily against outsiders but against those whom they saw as betraying and degrading Islam from within: on the one hand those who attempted any kind of modernizing reform; on the other—and this was the more immediate target—those whom the Wahhabis saw as corrupting and debasing the true Islamic heritage of the Prophet and his Companions. They were of course strongly opposed to any school or version of Islam, whether Sunni or Shi'ite, other than their own. They were particularly opposed to Sufism, condemning not only its mysticism and tolerance but also what they saw as the pagan cults associated with it.

Wherever they could, they enforced their beliefs with the utmost severity and ferocity, demolishing tombs, desecrating what they called false and idolatrous holy places, and slaughtering large numbers of men, women, and children who failed to meet their standards of Islamic purity and authenticity. Another practice introduced by Ibn 'Abd al-Wahhab was the condemnation and burning of books. These consisted mainly of Islamic works on theology and law deemed contrary to Wahhabi doctrine. The burning of books was often accompanied by the summary execution of those who wrote, copied, or taught them.

The second alliance of Wahhabi doctrine and Saudi force began in the last years of the Ottoman Empire and has continued to the present day. Two developments in the early twentieth century transformed Wahhabism into a major force in the Islamic world and beyond. The first of these was the expansion and consolidation of the Saudi kingdom. In the last years of the Ottoman Empire, Sheikh 'Abd al-'Aziz Ibn Saud (born ca. 1880, ruled 1902–1953) played skillfully on the struggle between the Ottomans on the one hand and the expanding British power in eastern Arabia on the other. In December 1915 he signed an agreement with Britain whereby, while preserving his independence, he obtained a subsidy and a promise of assistance if attacked. The end of the war and the breakup of the Ottoman Empire ended this phase, and left him face to face with Britain alone. He fared very well in this new arrangement and was able to expand his inherited realm in successive stages. In 1921 he finally defeated his longtime rival Ibn Rashid in Northern Najd and, annexing his territories, assumed the title sultan of Najd.

The stage was now set for a more crucial struggle, for control of the Hijaz. This land, including the two Muslim holy cities of Mecca and Medina, had been ruled by members of the Hashimite dynasty, descendants of the Prophet, for more than a millennium, in the last few centuries under loose Ottoman suzerainty. The establishment of Hashimite monarchies, headed by various branches of the family, in Iraq and in Transjordan as part of the restructuring of the former Ottoman Arab provinces after the First World War, was seen by Ibn Saud as a threat to his own realm. After years of worsening relations, King Hussein of the Hijaz provided a double pretext, first by proclaiming himself as caliph, second by refusing to allow Wahhabi pilgrims to perform the pilgrimage to the holy cities. Ibn Saud responded by invading the Hijaz in 1925.

The Saudis' war of conquest was a complete success. Their forces first captured Mecca; then, on December 5, 1925, after a siege of ten months, Medina surrendered peacefully. Two weeks later King 'Ali, who had succeeded his father, Hussein, asked the British vice consul in Jedda to inform Ibn Saud of his withdrawal from the Hijaz with his personal effects. This was taken as an abdication, and on the following day the Saudi forces entered Jedda. The way was now open for Ibn Saud to proclaim himself King of the Hijaz and Sultan of Najd and its Dependencies on January

8, 1926. The new regime was immediately recognized by the European powers, notably by the Soviet Union in a diplomatic note of February 16 to Ibn Saud, "on the basis of the principle of the people's right to self-determination and out of respect for the Hijazi people's will as expressed in their choice of you as their king."[1] A formal treaty between Ibn Saud and Great Britain, recognizing the full independence of the kingdom, was signed on May 20, 1927. Some other European states followed suit.

Muslim recognition in contrast was slower and more reluctant. A Muslim mission from India visited Jedda and demanded that the king hand over control of the holy cities to a committee of representatives to be appointed by all Muslim countries. Ibn Saud did not respond to this demand and sent the mission back to India by sea. In June of the same year, he convened an all-Islamic Congress in Mecca, inviting the sovereigns and presidents of the independent Muslim states and representatives from Muslim organizations in countries under non-Muslim rule. Sixty-nine people attended the congress from all over the Islamic world. Addressing them, Ibn Saud made it clear that he was now the ruler of the Hijaz. He would fulfill his duties as custodian of the holy places and protector of the pilgrimage but would not permit any outside intervention in his performance of these tasks.

At the time he evoked a mixed response from his guests. Some dissented and departed; others accepted and recognized the new order. Notable among the latter was the head of the delegation of Muslims in the Soviet Union, whose leader, in an interview with the Soviet news agency TASS, announced that this Islamic Congress had recognized King

Ibn Saud as Custodian of the Holy Places; it had also called for the transfer of parts of Jordan to the new Hijazi kingdom, and in general expressed support for Ibn Saud. Recognition from Muslim states and still more from Arab states took rather longer. Treaties of friendship were signed with Turkey and Iran in 1929, with Iraq in 1930, and with Jordan in 1933. The Saudi annexation of the Hijaz was not formally recognized by Egypt until the agreement of May 1936.

In the meantime, Ibn Saud proceeded rapidly with the reorganization and restructuring of his far-flung kingdom and in September 1932 proclaimed a new unitary state, to be called the Saudi Arabian Kingdom. In the following year he appointed his eldest son, Saud, as heir to the throne.

The same year saw the other major development affecting the region, with the signature, on May 19, 1933, of an agreement between the Saudi minister of finance and a representative of Standard Oil of California. Saudi politics and Wahhabi doctrines now rested on a solid financial foundation.

∾

Western interest in Middle Eastern oil dated from the early twentieth century and was mainly operated by British, Dutch, and French companies. American interest began in the early 1920s, with growing concern about the depletion of domestic oil resources and the fear of a European monopoly of Middle Eastern oil. American companies initially entered the Middle Eastern oil market as junior partners in European combines. Standard Oil of California was the first American company to undertake serious oil exploration. After some inconclusive efforts in the Gulf states, Standard Oil finally turned to the Saudis and in 1930 requested permission for a geological exploration of the eastern province. King Ibn Saud at first refused this request but then agreed to negotiations, which culminated in the agreement of 1933. One of the factors which induced the king to change his mind was no doubt the depression that began in 1929 and brought a serious and growing deterioration in the finances of the kingdom.

Less than four months after the signature of the agreement, the first American geologists arrived in eastern Arabia. By the end of the year, the exploratory mission was well established, and in the following year American teams began the extraction and export of oil. The process of development was interrupted by the Second World War but was resumed when the war ended. Some indication of the scale of development may be seen in the figures for oil extracted in Arabia, in millions of barrels: 1945, 21.3; 1955, 356.6; 1965, 804.8; 1975, 2,582.5.

The outward flow of oil and the corresponding inward flow of money brought immense changes to the Saudi kingdom, its internal structure and way of life, and its external role and influence, both in the oil-consuming countries and, more powerfully, in the world of Islam. The most significant change was in the impact of Wahhabism and the role of its protagonists. Wahhabism was now the official, state-enforced doctrine of one of the most influential governments in all Islam—the custodian of the two holiest places of Islam, the host of the annual pilgrimage, which brings millions of Muslims from every part of the world to share in its rites and rituals. At the same time, the teachers and preachers of Wahhabism had at their disposal immense financial resources, which they used to promote and spread their version of Islam. Even in Western countries in Europe and America, where the public educational systems are good, Wahhabi indoctrination centers may be the only form of Islamic education available to new converts and to Muslim parents who wish to give their children some grounding in their own inherited religious and cultural tradition. This indoctrination is provided in private schools, religious seminars, mosque schools, holiday camps and, increasingly, prisons.

In traditional Islamic usage the term *madrasa* denoted a center of higher education, of scholarship, teaching, and research. The classical Islamic madrasa was the predecessor of and in many ways the model for the great medieval European universities. In modern usage the word madrasa has acquired a negative meaning; it has come to denote a center for indoctrination in bigotry and violence. A revealing example may be seen in the backgrounds of a number of Turks arrested on suspicion of complicity in terrorist activities. Every single one of them was born and educated in Germany, not one in Turkey. The German government does not supervise the religious education of minority groups. The Turkish government keeps a watchful eye on these matters. In Europe and America, because of the reluctance of the state to involve itself in religious matters, the teaching of Islam in schools and elsewhere has in general been totally unsupervised by authority. This situation clearly favors those with the fewest scruples, the strongest convictions, and the most money.

The result can perhaps be depicted through an imaginary parallel. Imagine that the Ku Klux Klan or some similar group obtains total control of the state of Texas, of its oil and therefore of its oil revenues, and having done so, uses this money to establish a network of well-endowed schools and colleges all over Christendom, peddling their peculiar brand of Christianity. This parallel is somewhat less dire than the reality, since most Christian countries have functioning public school systems of their own. In some Muslim countries this is not so, and the Wahhabi-sponsored schools and colleges represent for many young Muslims the only education available. By these means the Wahhabis have carried their message all over the Islamic world and, increasingly, to Islamic minority communities in other countries, notably in Europe and North America. Organized Muslim public life, education, and even worship are, to an alarming extent, funded and therefore directed by Wahhabis, and the version of Islam that they practice and preach is dominated by Wahhabi principles and attitudes. The custodianship of the holy places and the revenues of oil have given worldwide impact to what would otherwise have been an extremist fringe in a marginal country.

~

The exploitation of oil brought vast new wealt~ ~it new and increasingly bitter social tensior~ society inequalities of wealth had been li~ effects were restrained—on the one hand~ social bonds and obligations that linke~ on the other hand, by the privacy~

...ization has all too often widened the gap, destroyed ...social bonds, and through the universality of the ...dern media, made the resulting inequalities painfully visible. All this has created new and receptive audiences for Wahhabi teachings and those of like-minded groups, among them the Muslim Brothers in Egypt and Syria and the Taliban in Afghanistan.

Oil wealth also had negative political effects, by inhibiting the development of representative institutions. "No taxation without representation" marks a crucial step in the development of Western democracy. Unfortunately, the converse is also true—no representation without taxation. Governments with oil wealth have no need for popular assemblies to impose and collect taxes, and can afford, for some time at least, to disregard public opinion. Even that term has little meaning in such societies. Lacking any other outlet, new and growing discontents also find expression in religious extremist movements.

It has now become normal to describe these movements as fundamentalist. The term is unfortunate for a number of reasons. It was originally an American Protestant term, used to designate certain Protestant churches that differed in some respects from the mainstream churches. The two main differences were liberal theology and biblical criticism, both seen as objectionable. Liberal theology has been an issue among Muslims in the past and may be again in the future. It is not at the present time. The literal divinity and inerrancy of the Qur'an is a basic dogma of Islam, and although some may doubt it, none challenge it. These dif-...rences bear no resemblance to those that divide Muslim ...ntalists from the Islamic mainstream, and the term can therefore be misleading. It is however now common usage, and has even been translated literally into Arabic, Persian, and Turkish.

The eclipse of pan-Arabism left Islamic fundamentalism as the most attractive alternative to all those who felt that there has to be something better, truer, and more hopeful than the inept tyrannies of their rulers and the bankrupt ideologies foisted on them from outside. These movements feed on privation and humiliation and on the frustration and resentments to which they give rise, after the failure of all the political and economic nostrums, both the foreign imports and the local imitations. As seen by many in the Middle East and north Africa, both capitalism and socialism were tried and have failed; both Western and Eastern models produced only poverty and tyranny. It may seem unjust that in post-independence Algeria, for example, the West should be blamed for the pseudo-Stalinist policies of an anti-Western government, for the failure of the one and the ineptitude of the other. But popular sentiment is not entirely wrong in seeing the Western world and Western ideas as the ultimate source of the major changes that have transformed the Islamic world in the last century or more. As a consequence, much of the anger in the Islamic world is directed against the Westerner, seen as the ancient and immemorial enemy of Islam since the first clashes between the Muslim caliphs and the Christian emperors, and against the Westernizer, seen as a tool or accomplice of the West and as a traitor to his own faith and people.

Religious fundamentalism enjoys several advantages against competing ideologies. It is readily intelligible to both educated and uneducated Muslims. It offers a set of themes, slogans, and symbols that are profoundly familiar and therefore effective in mobilizing support and in formulating both a critique of what is wrong and a program for putting it right. Religious movements enjoy another practical advantage in societies like those of the Middle East and north Africa that are under more or less autocratic rule: dictators can forbid parties, they can forbid meetings—they cannot forbid public worship, and they can to only a limited extent control sermons.

As a result the religious opposition groups are the only ones that have regular meeting places where they can assemble and have at their disposal a network outside the control of the state or at least not fully subject to it. The more oppressive the regime, the more it helps the fundamentalists by giving them a virtual monopoly of opposition.

Militant Islamic radicalism is not new. Several times since the beginnings of the Western impact in the eighteenth century, there have been religiously expressed militant opposition movements. So far they have all failed. Sometimes they have failed in an easy and relatively painless way by being defeated and suppressed, in which case the crown of martyrdom brought them a kind of success. Sometimes they have failed the hard way, by gaining power, and then having to confront great economic and social problems for which they had no real answers. What has usually happened is that they have become, in time, as oppressive and as cynical as their ousted predecessors. It is in this phase that they can become really dangerous, when, to use a European typology, the revolution enters the Napoleonic or, perhaps one should say, the Stalinist phase. In a program

of aggression and expansion these movements would enjo
like their Jacobin and Bolshevik predecessors, the advantage of fifth columns in every country and community with
which they share a common universe of discourse.

Broadly speaking, Muslim fundamentalists are those
who feel that the troubles of the Muslim world at the present time are the result not of insufficient modernization but
of excessive modernization, which they see as a betrayal of
authentic Islamic values. For them the remedy is a return to
true Islam, including the abolition of all the laws and other
social borrowings from the West and the restoration of the
Islamic Holy Law, the shari'a, as the effective law of the
land. From their point of view, the ultimate struggle is not
against the Western intruder but against the Westernizing
traitor at home. Their most dangerous enemies, as they see
it, are the false and renegade Muslims who rule the countries of the Islamic world and who have imported and
imposed infidel ways on Muslim peoples.

The point is clearly made in a tract by 'Abd al-Salām
Faraj, an Egyptian who was executed along with others in
April 1982 on the charge of having plotted and instigated
the assassination of President Sadat. His remarks throw
some light on the motivation of that act:

The basis of the existence of imperialism in the lands of
Islam is these self-same rulers. To begin with the struggle
against imperialism is a work which is neither glorious
nor useful, and it is only a waste of time. It is our duty to
concentrate on our Islamic cause, and that is the establishment first of all of God's law in our own country and
causing the word of God to prevail. There is no doubt

that the first battlefield of the jihad is the extirpation of these infidel leaderships and their replacement by a perfect Islamic order, and from this will come the release of our energies.[2]

In the few moments that passed between the murder of President Sadat and the arrest of his murderers, their leader exclaimed triumphantly: "I have killed Pharaoh! I am not afraid to die." If, as was widely assumed in the Western world at the time, Sadat's offense in the eyes of the murderers was making peace with Israel, Pharaoh would seem a singularly inappropriate choice of epithet. Clearly, they were not referring to the Pharaoh of modern Egyptian schoolbooks, the embodiment of the greatness and glory of ancient Egypt. It is the Pharaoh of the Exodus, who, in the Qur'an as in the Bible, is the pagan tyrant who oppresses God's people. It is no doubt in this sense that Usama bin Ladin spoke of President Bush as the Pharaoh of our day. At the time of the Exodus, the Children of Israel were God's people. Present-day Muslims for the most part do not recognize the modern State of Israel as the legitimate heir of the ancient Children of Israel—in the Qur'an *Banū Isrā'īl*— and the assassins of Sadat certainly did not approve of his deal with that state. But as the subsequent interrogation of the murderers and their accomplices made clear, the peace with Israel was, in their eyes, a relatively minor phenomenon—a symptom rather than a cause of the greater offense of abandoning God's faith, oppressing God's people, and aping the ways of the infidel.

# IX

## The Rise of Terrorism

Most Muslims are not fundamentalists, and most fundamentalists are not terrorists, but most present-day terrorists are Muslims and proudly identify themselves as such. Understandably, Muslims complain when the media speak of terrorist movements and actions as "Islamic" and ask why the media do not similarly identify Irish and Basque terrorists and terrorism as "Christian." The answer is simple and obvious—they do not describe themselves as such. The Muslim complaint is understandable, but it should be addressed to those who make the news, not to those who report it. Usama bin Ladin and his Al-Qaʻida followers may not represent Islam, and many of their statements and their actions directly contradict basic Islamic principles and teachings, but they do arise from within Muslim civilization, just as Hitler and the Nazis arose from within Christendom, and they too must be seen in their own cultural, religious, and historical context.

There are several forms of Islamic extremism current at the present time. The best known are the subversive radicalism of Al-Qaʻida and other groups that resemble it all over the Muslim world; the preemptive fundamentalism of the Saudi establishment; and the institutionalized revolution of the ruling Iranian hierarchy. All of these are, in a sense, Islamic in origin, but some of them have deviated very far from their origins.

All these different extremist groups sanctify their action through pious references to Islamic texts, notably the Qur'an and the traditions of the Prophet, and all three claim to represent a truer, purer, and more authentic Islam than that currently practiced by the vast majority of Muslims and endorsed by most though not all of the religious leadership. They are, however, highly selective in their choice and interpretation of sacred texts. In considering the sayings of the Prophet, for example, they discard the time-honored methods developed by the jurists and theologians for testing the accuracy and authenticity of orally transmitted traditions, and instead accept or reject even sacred texts according to whether they support or contradict their own dogmatic and militant positions. Some even go so far as to dismiss some Qur'anic verses as "revoked" or "abrogated." The argument used to justify this is that verses revealed during the early years of the Prophet's mission may be superseded by later, presumably more mature revelations.

A revealing example of such deviation was the famous fatwa issued by the Ayatollah Khomeini on February 14, 1989, against the novelist Salman Rushdie because of his novel entitled *The Satanic Verses*. In the fatwa, the Ayatollah informed "all the zealous Muslims of the world that the blood of the author of this book . . . which has been compiled, printed, and published in opposition to Islam, the Prophet, and the Qur'an, as also of those involved in its publication who were aware of its contents, is hereby declared forfeit. I call on all zealous Muslims to dispatch them quickly, wherever they may be found, so that no one will dare to insult Islamic sanctities again. Anyone who is himself killed in this path will be deemed a martyr."[1] To supplement and anticipate the rewards of paradise, an Islamic charitable trust in Tehran offered a bounty to anyone who killed Salman Rushdie consisting of 20 million *tumans* (at that time about $3 million at the official rate, about $170,000 at the open-market rate) for an Iranian, or $1 million for a foreigner. Some years later the bounty, still unclaimed, was increased by the trust.

Not surprisingly, many uninformed readers in the Western world got the impression that "to issue a fatwa" was the Islamic equivalent of "to put out a contract"—i.e., to target a victim and offer a monetary reward for murdering him. Like madrasa, the word fatwa has acquired, in common international usage, a wholly negative connotation. This is in fact a monstrous absurdity. Fatwa is a technical term in Islamic jurisprudence for a legal opinion or ruling on a point of law. It is the shariʿa equivalent of the *responsa prudentium* of Roman law. The Islamic jurisconsult who is authorized to issue a fatwa is called a mufti, an active participle from the same root. In using a fatwa to pronounce a death sentence and recruit an assassin, the ayatollah was deviating very considerably from standard Islamic practice.

The deviation was not only in the verdict and sentence but also in the nature of the charge. Insulting the Prophet— the charge brought against Salman Rushdie—is certainly an offense in Muslim law, and the jurists discuss it in some detail. Almost all these discussions turn on the question of a non-Muslim subject of the Muslim state who insults the

Prophet. The jurists devote considerable attention to the definition of the offense, the rules of evidence, and the appropriate punishment. They show great concern that accusations of this offense should not be used as a device to achieve some private vengeance, and insist on careful scrutiny of the evidence before any verdict or sentence is pronounced. The majority opinion is that a flogging and a term of imprisonment are sufficient punishment—the severity of the flogging and the length of the term to depend on the gravity of the offense. The case of the Muslim who insults the Prophet is hardly considered and must have been very rare. When it is discussed, the usual view is that this act is tantamount to apostasy.

This was the specific charge brought against Salman Rushdie. Apostasy is a major offense in Muslim law and for men carries the death penalty. But the important word in this statement is *law*. Islamic jurisprudence is a system of law and justice, not of lynching and terror. It lays down procedures according to which a person accused of an offense is to be brought to trial, confronted with his accuser, and given the opportunity to defend himself. A judge will then give a verdict and, if he finds the accused guilty, pronounce sentence.

There is however another view, held by a minority of jurists, that the offense committed by a Muslim who insults the Prophet is so great that one may, indeed must, dispense with the formalities of arraignment, trial, and conviction, and proceed directly with the execution. The basis of this view is a saying ascribed to the Prophet but by no means universally accepted as authentic: "If anyone insults me, then any Muslim who hears this must kill him immediately." Even among the jurists who accept the authenticity of this saying, there is disagreement. Some insist that some form of procedure or authorization is required, and that summary killing without such authorization is murder and should be punished as such. Others argue that the text of the saying as transmitted makes it clear that the summary and immediate execution of the blasphemer is not only lawful but obligatory, and that those who do not do it are themselves committing an offense. Even the most rigorous and extreme of the classical jurists only require a Muslim to kill anyone who insults the Prophet in his hearing and in his presence. They say nothing about a hired killing for a reported insult in a distant country.

The sanctification of murder embodied in Khomeini's fatwa appears in an even more advanced form in the practice—and the cult—of the suicide murderer.

≈

If one looks at the historical record, the Muslim approach to war does not differ greatly from that of Christians, or that of Jews in the very ancient and very modern periods when this option was open to them. While Muslims, perhaps more frequently than Christians, made war against the followers of other faiths to bring them within the scope of Islam, Christians—with the notable exception of the Crusades—were more prone to fight internal religious wars against those whom they saw as schismatics or heretics. Islam, no doubt owing to the political and military involvement of its Founder, takes what one might call a more pragmatic view than the Gospels of the realities of societal and state relationships. Its position is nearer to that of the earlier books of the Old Testament, and to the doctrine of smiting the Amalekites, rather than to the Prophets and the Gospels. Muslims are not instructed to turn the other cheek, nor do they expect to beat their swords into plowshares and their spears into pruning hooks (Isaiah 2:4). These injunctions did not of course prevent Christians from waging a series of bloody wars of religion within Christendom and wars of aggression outside.

This raises the larger issue of the attitude of religions to force and violence, and more specifically to terrorism. Followers of many faiths have at one time or another invoked religion in the practice of murder, both retail and wholesale. Two words deriving from such movements in Eastern religions have even entered the English language: *thug*, from India, and *assassin*, from the Middle East, both commemorating fanatical religious sects whose form of worship was to murder those they regarded as enemies of the faith.

The practice and then the theory of assassination in the Islamic world arose at a very early date, with disputes over the political headship of the Muslim community. Of the first four caliphs of Islam, three were murdered, the second by a disgruntled Christian slave, the third and fourth by pious Muslim rebels who saw themselves as executioners carrying out the will of God. The question arose in an acute form in 656 C.E., with the murder of the third caliph, 'Uthman, by Muslim rebels. The first of a succession of civil wars was fought over the question of whether the killers were fulfilling or defying God's commandment. Islamic law and tradition are very clear on the duty of obedience to the

Islamic ruler. But they also quote two sayings attributed to the Prophet: "There is no obedience in sin" and "Do not obey a creature against his creator." If a ruler orders something that is contrary to the law of God, then the duty of obedience is replaced by a duty of disobedience. The notion of tyrannicide—the justified removal of a tyrant—was not an Islamic innovation; it was familiar in antiquity, among Jews, Greeks, and Romans alike, and those who performed it were often acclaimed as heroes.

Members of the Muslim sect known as the Assassins (from the Arabic *Hashīshiyya*), active in Iran and then in Syria from the eleventh to the thirteenth century, seem to have been the first to transform the act that was named after them into a system and an ideology. Their efforts, contrary to popular belief, were primarily directed not against the Crusaders but against Muslim rulers, whom they saw as impious usurpers. In this sense, the Assassins are the true predecessors of many of the so-called Islamic terrorists of today, some of whom explicitly make this point. The name *Hashīshiyya,* with its connotation of "hashish taker," was given to them by their Muslim enemies. They called themselves *fidayeen*, from the Arabic *fidā'ī*—one who is ready to sacrifice his life for the cause.

After the defeat and suppression of the Assassins in the thirteenth century, the term passed out of use. It was briefly revived in the mid-nineteenth century, by a small group of Turkish conspirators who plotted to depose and perhaps assassinate the sultan. The plot was discovered and the conspirators imprisoned. The term reappeared in Iran, in the so-called Fida'iyan-i Islam, the *fidā'īs* of Islam, a political-religious terrorist group in Tehran, which between 1943, when it began its activities, and 1955, when it was suppressed, carried out a number of political assassinations. After an unsuccessful attempt on the life of the prime minister in October 1955, they were arrested, prosecuted, and their leaders executed. The term was revived again by the militant wing of the Palestine Liberation Organization and, from the 1960s onward, designated terrorist activists of the Palestinian organizations.

In two respects, in their choice of weapons and in their choice of victims, the Assassins were markedly different from their present-day successors. The victim was always an individual, a highly placed political, military, or religious leader who was seen as the source of evil. He, and he alone, was killed. This action was not terrorism in the current sense of that term but rather what is now called targeted assassination. The weapon was always the same: the dagger. The Assassins disdained poison, crossbows, and other weapons that could be used from a distance, and the Assassin did not expect—or, it would seem, even desire—to survive his act, which he believed would ensure him eternal bliss. But in no circumstance did he commit suicide. He died at the hands of his captors. The Assassins were finally defeated by military expeditions which captured their strongholds and bases in both Iran and Syria, the two countries in which they principally operated. It may well be that the present-day assassins will be similarly defeated, but it will be a long and hard road. The medieval Assassins were an extremist sect, very far from mainstream Islam. That is not true of their present-day imitators.

~

The twentieth century brought a renewal of such actions in the Middle East, though of different types and for different purposes, and terrorism has gone through several phases. During the last years of the British Empire, imperial Britain faced terrorist movements in its Middle Eastern dependencies that represented three different cultures: Greeks in Cyprus, Jews in Palestine, and Arabs in Aden. All three acted from nationalist, rather than religious, motives. Though very different in their backgrounds and political circumstances, the three were substantially alike in their tactics. Their purpose was to persuade the imperial power that staying in the region was not worth the cost in blood. Their method was to attack military and, to a lesser extent, administrative personnel and installations. All three operated only within their own territory and generally avoided collateral damage. All three succeeded in their endeavors.

For the new-style terrorists, the slaughter of innocent and uninvolved civilians is not "collateral damage." It is the prime objective. Inevitably, the counterattack against the terrorists—who do not of course wear uniforms—also targets civilians. The resulting blurring of distinctions is immensely useful to the terrorists and to their sympathizers.

Thanks to the rapid development of the media, and especially of television, the more recent forms of terrorism are aimed not at specific and limited enemy objectives but at world opinion. Their primary purpose is not to defeat or even to weaken the enemy militarily but to gain publicity and to inspire fear—a psychological victory. The same kind of terrorism was practiced by a number of European groups, notably in Germany, Italy, Spain, and Ireland. Among the most successful and most enduring in this exercise has been the Palestine Liberation Organization.

The PLO was founded in 1964 but became important in 1967, after the defeat of the combined Arab armies in the Six-Day War. Regular warfare had failed; it was time to try other methods. The targets in this form of armed struggle were not military or other government establishments, which are usually too well guarded, but public places and gatherings of any kind, which are overwhelmingly civilian and in which the victims do not necessarily have a connection to the declared enemy. Examples of this tactic include, in 1970, the hijacking of three aircraft—one Swiss, one British, and one American—which were all taken to Amman; the 1972 murder of Israeli athletes at the Munich Olympics; the seizure in 1973 of the Saudi Embassy in Khartoum and the murder there of two Americans and a Belgian diplomat; the takeover of the Italian cruise ship *Achille Lauro,* in 1985, and the murder of a crippled passenger. Other attacks were directed against schools, shopping malls, discotheques, and even passengers waiting in line at European airports. These and other operations by the PLO were remarkably successful in attaining their immediate objective—the capture of newspaper headlines and television screens. They also drew a great deal of support in sometimes unexpected places, and raised their perpetrators to starring roles in the drama of international relations. Small wonder that others were encouraged to follow their example. The Arab terrorists of the 1970s and 1980s made it clear that they were waging a war for an Arab or Palestinian national cause, not for Islam. Indeed, a significant proportion of the PLO leaders and activists were Christian.

But despite its media successes, the Palestine Liberation Organization achieved no significant results where it mattered—in Palestine. In every Arab land but Palestine, the nationalists achieved their purposes—the defeat and departure of foreign rulers and the establishment of national sovereignty under national leaders.

For a while, freedom and independence were used as more or less synonymous and interchangeable terms. The early experience of independence, however, revealed that this was a sad error. Independence and freedom are very different, and all too often the attainment of one meant the end of the other, and the replacement of foreign overlords by domestic tyrants, more adept, more intimate, and less constrained in their tyranny.

There was an urgent, growing need for a new explanation of what was wrong, and a new strategy for putting it right. Both were found, in religious feeling and identity. This choice was not new. In the first half of the nineteenth century, when the European empires were advancing on many of the lands of Islam, the most significant resistance to their advance was religiously inspired and defined. The French in Algeria, the Russians in the Caucasus, the British in India all faced major religious uprisings, which they overcame only after long and bitter fights.

A new phase in religious mobilization began with the movement known in Western languages as pan-Islamism. Launched in the 1860s and '70s, it probably owed something to the examples of the Germans and the Italians in their successful struggles for national unification in those years. Their Muslim contemporaries and imitators inevitably identified themselves and defined their objectives in religious and communal rather than nationalist or patriotic terms, which at that time were still alien and unfamiliar. But with the spread of European influence and education, these ideas took root and for a while dominated both discourse and struggle in the Muslim lands. Yet the religious identity and loyalty were still deeply felt, and they found expression in several religious movements, notably the Muslim Brothers. With the resounding failure of secular ideologies, they acquired a new importance, and these movements took over the fight—and many of the fighters— from the failed nationalists.

For the fundamentalists as for the nationalists, the various territorial issues are important but in a different, more intractable form. For example, for the fundamentalists in general, no peace or compromise with Israel is possible, and any concession is only a step toward the true final solution—the dissolution of the State of Israel, the return of the land to its true owners, the Muslim Palestinians, and the death or departure of the intruders. Yet this would by no means satisfy the fundamentalists' demands, which extend to all the other disputed territories—and even their acquisition would only be a step toward the longer, final struggle.

Much of the old tactic was retained, but in a significantly more vigorous form. Both in defeat and in victory, the religious terrorists adopted and improved on the methods pioneered by the nationalists of the twentieth century, in particular the lack of concern at the slaughter of innocent bystanders. This unconcern reached new proportions in the terror campaign launched by Usama bin Ladin in the early 1990s. The first major example was the bombing of two American embassies in East Africa in 1998. In order to kill twelve American diplomats, the terrorists were willing to slaughter more than two hundred Africans, many of them Muslims, who happened to be in the vicinity. In its issue immediately after these attacks, an Arabic-language fundamentalist magazine called *Al-Sirāt al-Mustaqīm,* published in Pittsburgh, Pennsylvania, expressed its mourning for the "martyrs" who gave their lives in these operations and listed their names, as supplied by the office of Al-Qa'ida in Peshawar, Pakistan. The writer added an expression of hope "that God would . . . reunite us with them in paradise." The same disregard for human life, on a vastly greater scale, underlay the actions in New York and Washington on September 11, 2001.

❧

A significant figure in these operations was the suicide terrorist. In one sense, this was a new development. The nationalist terrorists of the 1960s and '70s generally took care not to die along with their victims but arranged to carry out their attacks from a safe distance. If they had the misfortune to be captured, their organizations usually tried, sometimes successfully, to obtain their release by seizing hostages and threatening to harm or kill them. Earlier religiously inspired murderers, notably the Assassins, disdained to survive their operations but did not actually kill themselves. The same may be said of the Iranian boy soldiers in the 1980–1988 war against Iraq, who walked through minefields, armed only with a passport to paradise, to clear the way for the regular troops.

The new type of suicide mission in the strict sense of the word seems to have been pioneered by religious organizations like Hamas and Hizbullah, who from 1982 onward carried out a number of such missions in Lebanon and in Israel. They continued through the 1980s and '90s, with echoes in other areas, for example in eastern Turkey, in Egypt, in India, and in Sri Lanka. From the information available, it would seem that the candidates chosen for these missions were, with occasional exceptions, male, young, and poor, often from refugee camps. They were offered a double reward—in the afterlife, the minutely described delights of paradise; in this world, bounties and stipends for their families. A remarkable innovation was the use of female suicide bombers—by Kurdish terrorists in Turkey in 1996–1999, and by Palestinians from January 2002.

Unlike the medieval holy warrior or assassin, who was willing to face certain death at the hands of his enemies or captors, the new suicide terrorist dies by his own hand. This raises an important question of Islamic teaching. Islamic law books are very clear on the subject of suicide. It is a major sin and is punished by eternal damnation in the form of the endless repetition of the act by which the suicide killed himself. The following passages, from the traditions of the Prophet, make the point vividly:

> The Prophet said: Whoever kills himself with a blade will be tormented with that blade in the fires of Hell.
>
> The Prophet also said: He who strangles himself will

strangle himself in Hell, and he who stabs himself will stab himself in Hell. . . . He who throws himself off a mountain and kills himself will throw himself downward into the fires of Hell for ever and ever. He who drinks poison and kills himself will carry his poison in his hand and drink it in Hell for ever and ever. . . . Whoever kills himself in any way will be tormented in that way in Hell. . . . Whoever kills himself in any way in this world will be tormented with it on the day of resurrection.[2]

The early authorities make a clear distinction between facing certain death at the hands of the enemy and dying by one's own hand. A very early tradition of the type known as *hadīth qudsī*, denoting a statement of the Prophet citing God Himself, gives a striking example. The Prophet was present when a man mortally wounded in the holy war killed himself to shorten his pain. Whereupon God said: "My servant pre-empted me by taking his soul with his own hand; he will therefore not be admitted to paradise." According to another early tradition, the Prophet refused to say prayers over the body of a man who had died by his own hand.[3]

Two features mark the attacks of September 11 and other similar actions: the willingness of the perpetrators to commit suicide and the ruthlessness of those who send them, concerning both their own emissaries and their numerous victims. Can these in any sense be justified in terms of Islam?

The answer must be a clear no.

The callous destruction of thousands in the World Trade Center, including many who were not American, some of them Muslims from Muslim countries, has no justification in Islamic doctrine or law and no precedent in Islamic history. Indeed, there are few acts of comparable deliberate and indiscriminate wickedness in human history. These are not just crimes against humanity and against civilization; they are also acts—from a Muslim point of view—of blasphemy, when those who perpetrate such crimes claim to be doing so in the name of God, His Prophet, and His scriptures.

The response of many Arabs and Muslims to the attack on the World Trade Center was one of shock and horror at the terrible destruction and carnage, together with shame and anger that this was being done in their name and in the name of their faith. This was the response of many—but not all. There were reports and even pictures of rejoicing in the streets in Arab and other Muslim cities at the news from New York. In part, the reaction was one of envy—a sentiment that was also widespread, in a more muted form, in Europe. Among the poor and the wretched there was a measure of satisfaction—for some indeed of delight—in seeing the rich and self-indulgent Americans being taught a lesson.

Responses in the Arabic press to the massacres in New York and Washington were an uneasy balance between denial and approval, rather similar to their response to the Holocaust.[4] On the Holocaust three positions are not infrequently found in the Arabic media: it never happened; it was greatly exaggerated; the Jews deserved it anyway. On the last point, some more enterprising writers add a rebuke to Hitler for not having finished the job. No one has yet asserted that the destruction of the World Trade Center never happened, though with the passage of time this will not be beyond the capacity of conspiracy theorists. The present line among many though by no means all Muslim commentators is to argue that neither Muslims nor Arabs could have done this. Instead, they offer other explanations. These include American white supremacists and militias, with reference of course to Oklahoma and Timothy McVeigh; opponents of globalization; European, Chinese, and other opponents of the missile defense shield project; the Russians, seeking vengeance for the breakup of the Soviet Union; the Japanese, as a long-delayed reprisal for Hiroshima; and the like. One columnist even suggests that the attack was organized by President Bush, to distract attention from his election by "a minuscule minority that would not have sufficed to elect a village counselor in upper Egypt." This writer also implicates Colin Powell as an accomplice of both Presidents Bush.

By far the most popular explanation attributes the crime, with minor variations, to their favorite villains—to Israel, to the Mossad (according to some, in association with the CIA), to the Elders of Zion, or most simply and satisfactorily, to "the Jews." This enables them at once to appreciate and to disown the attacks. The motive ascribed to the Jews is to make the Arabs and more generally the Muslims look bad and to sow discord between them and the Americans. A Jordanian columnist added an interesting additional theme—that "the Zionist organizations" perpetrated the attack so that Israel could destroy the Aksa Mosque while the attention of the world was diverted to America. This kind of explanation does not inhibit—on the contrary, it encourages—the frequently expressed view that what happened, though criminal, was a just retribution for American crimes. Perhaps the most dramatic—and explicit—response came from the Hamas weekly, *Al-Risāla,* in Gaza, in its issue of September 13, 2001: "Allah has answered our prayers."

As the full horror of the operation became better known, some writers were willing to express condemnation of the perpetrators and compassion for the victims. But even these rarely missed the opportunity to point out that the Americans had brought it on themselves. The catalog of American offenses they cite is long and detailed, beginning with the conquest, colonization, and settlement—emotive words—of the New World and continuing to the present day; so too is the list of victims who have fallen prey to American greed and ruthlessness, in Asia, Africa, and Latin America.

Usama bin Ladin has made clear how he perceives the struggle by repeatedly defining his enemy as "Crusaders." The Crusaders, it will be recalled, were neither Americans nor Jews; they were Christians fighting a holy war to recover the lost holy places of Christendom. A "letter to America" published in November 2002,[5] and attributed to Usama bin Ladin, enumerates in some detail various offenses committed not just by the government but also by the people of the United States and sets forth, under seven headings, "what we are calling you to do, and what we want from you." The first is to embrace Islam; the second, "to stop your oppressions, lies, immorality, and debauchery"; the third, to discover and admit that America is "a nation without principles or manners"; the fourth, to stop supporting Israel in Palestine, the Indians in Kashmir, the

Russians against the Chechens, and the Manila government against the Muslims in the southern Philippines; the fifth, "to pack your luggage and get out of our lands." This is offered as advice for America's own good, "so do not force us to send you back as cargo in coffins." The sixth, "to end your support of the corrupt leaders in our countries. Do not interfere in our politics and method of education. Leave us alone, or else expect us in New York and Washington; seventh, to deal and interact with the Muslims on the basis of mutual interests and benefits, rather than the policies of subjugation, theft, and occupation." The document ends by telling the Americans that, if they reject this advice, they will be defeated like all the previous Crusaders, and "their fate will be that of the Soviets who fled from Afghanistan to deal with their military defeat, political breakup, ideological downfall, and economic bankruptcy."

The case against America made in this document is very detailed. It includes, apart from the familiar list of specific grievances, a range of accusations both general and particular. These are of varied and usually recognizable provenance, reflecting the successive ideologies that have at different times influenced Middle Eastern politicians and policies. Some date from the Nazi era, e.g., degeneracy and ultimate Jewish control; others from the period of Soviet influence, e.g., capitalist greed and exploitation. Many are of recent European and even American origin, and come from both left and right. They include world pollution and the refusal to sign the Kyoto accords; political corruption through campaign financing; privileging the "white race"; and, from the right, the neo-Nazi, white supremacist myth that Benjamin Franklin gave warning against the Jewish danger. The sinister role of the Jews is stressed in almost all these offenses.

Even the vaunted merits of the American way of life become crimes and sins. The liberation of women means debauchery and the commercial use of women as "consumer products." Free elections mean that the American people freely chose their rulers and must therefore be held accountable and punishable for those rulers' misdeeds—that is, there are no "innocent civilians." Worst of all is the separation of church and state: "You are the nation who, rather than ruling by the Shariah of Allah in its Constitution and Laws, choose to invent your own laws as you will and desire. You separate religion from your policies, contradicting the pure nature which affirms Absolute Authority to the Lord and your Creator." In sum, "You are the worst civilization witnessed by the history of mankind." This judgment is the more remarkable coming at a time when the Nazi and Soviet dictatorships are still living memories—not to speak of earlier tyrannies preserved in the historical record which Usama bin Ladin and his associates so often cite.

The basic reason is that America is now perceived as the leader of what is variously designated as the West, Christendom, or more generally the "Lands of the Unbelievers." In this sense the American president is the successor of a long line of rulers—the Byzantine emperors of Constantinople, the Holy Roman emperors in Vienna, Queen Victoria and her imperial colleagues and successors in Europe. Today as in the past, this world of Christian unbelievers is seen as the only serious force rivaling and obstructing the divinely ordained spread of Islam, resisting and delaying but not preventing its final, inevitable, universal triumph.

There is no doubt that the foundation of Al-Qaʿida and the consecutive declarations of war by Usama bin Ladin marked the beginning of a new and ominous phase in the history of both Islam and terrorism. The triggers for bin Ladin's actions, as he himself has explained very clearly, were America's presence in Arabia during the Gulf War—a desecration of the Muslim Holy Land—and America's use of Saudi Arabia as a base for an attack on Iraq. If Arabia is the most symbolic location in the world of Islam, Baghdad, the seat of the caliphate for half a millennium and the scene of some of the most glorious chapters in Islamic history, is the second.

There was another, perhaps more important, factor driving bin Ladin. In the past, Muslims fighting against the West could always turn to the enemies of the West for comfort, encouragement, and material and military help. Now, for the first time in centuries, there is no such useful enemy. Bin Ladin and his cohorts soon realized that, in the new configuration of world power, if they wished to fight America they had to do it themselves. In 1991, the same year that the Soviet Union ceased to exist, bin Ladin and his cohorts created Al-Qaʿida, which included many veterans of the war in Afghanistan. Their task might have seemed daunting to anyone else, but they did not see it that way. In their view, they had already driven the Russians out of Afghanistan, in a defeat so overwhelming that it led directly to the collapse of the Soviet Union. Having overcome the superpower that they had always regarded as more formidable, they felt ready to take on the other; in this they were encouraged by the opinion, often expressed by bin Ladin among others, that America was a paper tiger.

Muslim terrorists had been driven by such beliefs before. One of the most surprising revelations in the memoirs of those who held the American Embassy in Tehran from 1979 to 1981 was that their original intention had been to hold the building and the hostages for only a few days. They changed their minds when statements from Washington made it clear that there was no danger of serious action against them. They finally released the hostages, they explained, only because they feared that the president-elect, Ronald Reagan, might approach the problem "like a cowboy." Bin Ladin and his followers clearly have no such concern, and their hatred is neither constrained by fear nor diluted by respect. As precedents, they repeatedly cite the American retreats from Vietnam, from Lebanon, and—the most important of all, in their eyes—from Somalia. Bin Ladin's remarks in an interview with John Miller, of ABC News, on May 28, 1998, are especially revealing:

> We have seen in the last decade the decline of the American government and the weakness of the American soldier, who is ready to wage cold wars and unprepared to fight long wars. This was proven in Beirut when the Marines fled after two explosions. It also proves they can run in less than twenty-four hours, and this was also repeated in Somalia. . . . [Our] youth were surprised at the low morale of the American soldiers. . . . After a few blows, they ran in defeat. . . . They forgot about being the world leader and the leader of the new world order.

[They] left, dragging their corpses and their shameful defeat.

For Usama bin Ladin, his declaration of war against the United States marks the resumption of the struggle for religious dominance of the world that began in the seventh century. For him and his followers, this is a moment of opportunity. Today, America exemplifies the civilization and embodies the leadership of the House of War, and like Rome and Byzantium, it has become degenerate and demoralized, ready to be overthrown. But despite its weakness, it is also dangerous. Khomeini's designation of the United States as "the Great Satan" was telling, and for the members of Al-Qa'ida it is the seduction of America and of its profligate, dissolute way of life that represents the greatest threat to the kind of Islam they wish to impose on their fellow Muslims.

But there are others for whom America offers a different kind of temptation—the promise of human rights, of free institutions, and of a responsible and representative government. There are a growing number of individuals and even some movements that have undertaken the complex task of introducing such institutions in their own countries. It is not easy. Similar attempts, as noted, led to many of today's corrupt regimes. Of the fifty-seven member states of the Organization of the Islamic Conference, only one, the Turkish Republic, has operated democratic institutions over a long period of time and, despite difficult and ongoing problems, has made progress in establishing a liberal economy and a free society and political order.

In two countries, Iraq and Iran, where the regimes are

strongly anti-American, there are democratic oppositions capable of taking over and forming governments. We, in what we like to call the free world, could do much to help them, and have done little. In most other countries in the region, there are people who share our values, sympathize with us, and would like to share our way of life. They understand freedom and want to enjoy it at home. It is more difficult for us to help those people, but at least we should not hinder them. If they succeed, we shall have friends and allies in the true, not just the diplomatic, sense of these words.

Meanwhile, there is a more urgent problem. If the leaders of Al-Qaʻida can persuade the world of Islam to accept their views and their leadership, then a long and bitter struggle lies ahead, and not only for America. Europe, more particularly Western Europe, is now home to a large and rapidly growing Muslim community, and many Europeans are beginning to see its presence as a problem, for some even a threat. Sooner or later, Al-Qaʻida and related groups will clash with the other neighbors of Islam—Russia, China, India—who may prove less squeamish than the Americans in using their power against Muslims and their sanctities. If the fundamentalists are correct in their calculations and succeed in their war, then a dark future awaits the world, especially the part of it that embraces Islam.

# Acknowledgments

The nucleus of this book was an article published in *The New Yorker,* in November 2001. In bringing it up to date and developing it from a long article to a short book, I have adapted a few passages from previous publications, especially some articles published in *Foreign Affairs* and *The Atlantic Monthly.* The rest is new.

There remains the pleasant task of thanking those who have been helpful in the preparation and production of this book. I am especially grateful once again to my relentless and invaluable editor, Joy de Menil, and to my assistant, Annamarie Cerminaro, for their unfailing support and help; to my friend Buntzie Churchill for her critical reading of my earlier drafts and her suggestions for their improvement; to Eli Alshech, a graduate student at Princeton who helped in various ways in the process of research and preparation. Any faults that remain are of course entirely my own.

# Afterword

The American military intervention in Afghanistan and then in Iraq has had two declared objectives: the first and more immediate, to deter and defeat terrorism; the second, to bring freedom, sometimes called democracy, to the peoples of these countries and beyond.

The sponsors and organizers of terrorism are of two kinds, with very different purposes, even though they can and frequently do cooperate. One of the two is local or regional, and consists of survivors of the former Iraqi regime, encouraged and supported by the governments of other countries in the region that feel endangered by what might happen in Iraq. The aim of these groups is to protect—or in the case of Iraq, restore—the tyrannies under which these countries have lived so long. If, as many urge, the Americans decide to abandon this costly and troublesome operation and simply go home, this might just possibly be enough to satisfy the local sponsors of terror. Some of them might even offer the hoped-for resumption of what passes for friendly relations.

The other group of terrorists would see the eviction of the Americans from Afghanistan and Iraq not as the end but as the beginning—as a victory not in a war but in a battle, one step in a longer and wider war that must be pursued until the final and global victory.

The Americans, too, have proclaimed a larger and longer purpose for their intervention; not just to defeat and end terrorism, but to give to the long-oppressed peoples of Afghanistan, Iraq, and eventually other countries the opportunity to end the corrupt and oppressive regimes under which they have suffered for decades and to restore or create a political order respected by and answerable to the people. This evokes strong support among many in the region. But, because of both past experience and current discourse, that support is understandably wary.

Certainly, the creation of a democracy in the Middle East will not be quick or easy, any more than it was in Europe or the Americas. There too it must come in gradual stages. Going too far too fast would give an immediate advantage to those skilled in the arts of manipulation and of intimidation. As the example of Algeria demonstrates, it can even lead to a violent clash between the two.

The kind of dictatorship that exists in the Middle East today has to no small extent been the result of modernization, more specifically of European influence and example. This included the only European political model that really worked in the Middle East—that of the one-party state, either in the Nazi or the Communist version, which did not differ greatly from one another. In these systems, the party is not, as in the West, an organization for attracting votes and winning elections; it is part of the apparatus of government, particularly concerned with indoctrination and enforcement. The Ba'th Party has a double ancestry, both Fascist and Communist, and still represents both trends very well.

But beyond these there are older traditions, well represented in both the political literature and the political experience of the Islamic Middle East: traditions of government under law, by consent, even by contract.

Changes in the spirit of these traditions would offer an

opportunity to other versions of Islam besides the fanatical and intolerant creed of the terrorists. Though at present widely held and richly endowed, this version is far from representative of mainstream Islam through the centuries. The traditions of command and obedience are indeed deep-rooted, but there are other elements in Islamic tradition that could contribute to a more open and freer form of government: the rejection by the traditional jurists of despotic and arbitrary rule in favor of contract in the formation and consensus in the conduct of government; their insistence that the mightiest of rulers, no less than the humblest of his servants, is bound by the law. Another is the acceptance, indeed the requirement of tolerance, embodied in such dicta as the Qur'anic verse 'there is no compulsion in religion,' and the early tradition: 'diversity in my community is God's mercy.' This is carried a step further in the Sufi ideal of dialogue between faiths in a common search for the fulfillment of shared aspirations.

The attempt to bring freedom to the Middle East evokes two fears: one in the United States and still more in Europe, that it will fail; the other, among many of the present rulers of the region, that it will succeed. Certainly, policies of political liberalization in Afghanistan and in Iraq offer a mortal threat to regimes that can survive only by tyranny at home and terror abroad. The enemies of freedom are dangerous, unrestrained by any kind of scruple, unhampered by either compunction or compassion, even for their own people. They are willing to use not just individuals and families, but whole nations as suicide bombers to be sacrificed as required in order to defeat and eject the infidel enemy and establish their own supremacy.

The creation of a free society, as the history of existing

democracies in the world makes clear, is no easy matter. The experience of the Turkish republic over the last half century and of some other Muslim countries more recently has demonstrated two things: first, that it is indeed very difficult to create a democracy in such a society, and second, that although difficult, it is not impossible. The study of Islamic history and of the vast and rich Islamic political literature encourages the belief that it may well be possible to develop democratic institutions—not necessarily in our Western definition of that much misused term but in one deriving from their own history and culture and ensuring, in their way, limited government under law, consultation and openness, in a civilized and humane society. There is enough in the traditional culture of Islam on the one hand and the modern experience of the Muslim peoples on the other to provide the basis for an advance toward freedom in the true sense of that word.

The forces of tyranny and terror are still very strong and the outcome is far from certain. But as the struggle rages and intensifies, certain things that were previously obscure are becoming clear. The war against terror and the quest for freedom are inextricably linked, and neither can succeed without the other. The struggle is no longer limited to one or two countries, as some Westerners still manage to believe. It has acquired first a regional then a global dimension, with profound consequences for all of us.

If freedom fails and terror triumphs, the peoples of Islam will be the first and greatest victims. They will not be alone, and many others will suffer with them.

December 1, 2003, Princeton, N.J.

# Notes

INTRODUCTION

1. The first of these names reappeared briefly in the late Ottoman period, when the province of Damascus was renamed province of Syria (Suriye). Its borders were significantly different from those of the postwar republic. The Roman-Byzantine name Palestine was retained for a while by the Arab conquerors but was already forgotten by the time the Crusaders arrived. It reappeared with the establishment of the British Mandate after the First World War. The Roman name Libya was unknown until it was officially reintroduced by the Italians.

2. Ibn Khaldūn, *Al-Muqaddima,* ed. E. Quatremère (Paris, 1858), vol. 1, p. 237.

CHAPTER II

1. These and other texts on jihad will be found in the standard collections of the traditions of the Prophet, some of which are also available in English translation. The above are taken from 'Alā' al-Dīn 'Alī ibn Ḥusām al-Dīn al-Muttaqī, *Kanz al-'Ummāl,* 8 parts (Hyderabad, 1312; 1894–1895), vol. 2, pp. 252–286.

CHAPTER III

1. Ibn al-Athīr, *Al-Kāmil fi'l-Ta'rīkh,* ed. C. J. Tornberg, vol. 11, year 583 (Leiden, 1853–1864), pp. 354–355.

2. Selaniki Mustafa Efendi, *Tarih-i Selaniki,* ed. Mehmet Ipşirli, Second Edition, Istanbul, 1999, p. 334.

3. Adolphus Slade, *Turkey and the Crimean War: A Narrative of Historical Events* (London, 1867), pp. 30–32.

4. For a slightly revised English version, see Snouck Hurgronje, *Verspreide Geschriften,* vol. 3 (Leiden, 1923), pp. 257 ff.

5. Anwar al-Sadat, *Al-Baḥth 'an al-dhāt* (Cairo, 1978), pp. 50–86; English version, *In Search of Identity, an Autobiography* (New York, 1978), pp. 31 ff.


CHAPTER IV

1. Muhammad ibn 'Uthmān al-Miknāsī (Moroccan ambassador in Spain, 1779 and 1788), *Al-Iksīr fī Fikāk al-Asīr,* ed. Muhammad al-Fāsī (Rabat, 1965), p. 97. See further Ami Ayalon, "The Arab Discovery of America in the Nineteenth Century," *Middle Eastern Studies,* vol. 20 (October 1984), pp. 5–17.

2. E. de Marcère, *Une Ambassade à Constantinople; la politique orientale de la Révolution française* (Paris, 1927), vol. 2, pp. 12–15.

3. Rifā'a Rāfi' al-Tahtāwī, *Qalā'id al-Mafākhir fī gharīb 'awā'id al-awā'il wa'l-awākhir* (Bulaq, 1833), p. 1, p. 14; cf. Ayalon, "Arab Discovery of America," p. 9.

4. Sayyid Qutb, *Al-Islām wa-mushkilāt al-hadāra* (n.p., 1967), pp. 80 ff. See also John Calvert, " 'The World is an Undutiful Boy!' Sayyid Qutb's American Experiences," in *Islam and Christian-Muslim Relations,* 2

(March 2000), pp. 87–103. He devoted a separate book, published posthumously in Saudi Arabia, to "our battle with the Jews": *Ma'rakatuna ma'a'l-Yahūd* ( Jedda, 1970). In addition to the specific Arab conflict with the Jews, he speaks of the pernicious Jewish role in the war against Islam and more generally against religious values: "Behind the atheist, materialist conception is a Jew—[Marx]; behind the bestial sexual conception, a Jew [Freud]; behind the destruction of the family and the disruption of the holy bonds of society, a Jew—[Durkheim]." The three are actually named not by Sayyid Qutb but by his editor, who for good measure adds a fourth in a footnote—Jean-Paul Sartre, made into a Jew for this purpose, as the inspirer of the literature of disintegration and ruin. It seems likely that Sayyid Qutb's inspiration for this and other anti-Jewish (as distinct from anti-Israel and anti-Zionist) passages was European or American.

CHAPTER V

1. These and other texts will be found in *Islam and Revolution: Writings and Declarations of Imam Khomeini,* translated and annotated by Hamid Algar (Berkeley, 1981). His *Islamic Government* was a series of lectures delivered in the Shi'ite center of Najaf, Iraq, Khomeini's place of exile, and published soon after in both Arabic and Persian. To those who read it, the subsequent course of the Islamic revolution in Iran will have come as no surprise.

2. On this treaty see Bernard Lewis, "Orientalist Notes on the Soviet–United Arab Republic Treaty of 27 May

1971," *Princeton Papers in Near Eastern Studies,* no. 2 (1993), pp. 57–65.

CHAPTER VII

1. *The Arab Human Development Report 2002: Creating Opportunities for Future Generations,* sponsored by the Regional Bureau for Arab States/UNDP, Arab Fund for Economic and Social Development.

CHAPTER VIII

1. Cited in Alexei Vassiliev, *The History of Saudi Arabia* (London, 1998), p. 265.
2. 'Abd al-Salām Faraj, *Al-Jihād: al-Farīda al-Ghā'iba* (Amman, 1982); English translation in Johannes J. G. Jansen, *The Neglected Duty: The Creed of Sadat's Assassins and Islamic Resurgence in the Middle East* (New York, 1986), pp. 159 ff.

CHAPTER IX

1. The full text of the fatwa was published in the Iranian and international press at the time.
2. These and similar traditions will be found in the standard collections of *hadīths,* for example, the *Sahīh* of al-Bukhārī, *Recueil des Traditions Mahométanes,* vol. 1, ed. M. Ludolf Krehl (Leiden, 1862), p. 363; vol. 2 (Leiden, 1864), pp. 223–224, 373; vol. 4, ed. Th. W. Juynboll (Leiden, 1908), pp. 71, 124, 243, 253–254, 320, 364. For a full discussion see Franz Rosenthal, "On Suicide in Islam," *Journal of the American Oriental Society,* vol. 66 (1946), pp. 239–259.

3. Cited inter alia by Ibn Hanbal, *Musnad* (Cairo, 1313; 1895–1896), vol. 5, p. 87.
4. For these and other reports on the Arabic media, see the Middle East Media Research Institute, Washington, D.C. (www.memri.org).
5. The full text of the letter, in both Arabic and English, was widely distributed via the Internet in November 2002. Because of differences of style and outlook, the personal authorship of Usama bin Ladin is unlikely.

3 Cited inter alia by Abu 'l-Faraj Harun, Mas'ud al-Gharb, 1134, Introduction, vol. 2, p. 8.

4 For these and other reports on the Arabic media, see the Middle East Media Research Institute, Washington, D.C. (www.memri.org).

5 The full text of the letter, in both Arabic and English, was widely distributed via the Internet in November 2002. Because of difference of style and outlook, the personal authorship of Usama bin Ladin is unlikely.

# Index

Abu Bakr (caliph), 6
Aden, 49, 125
Afghanistan, xxi, 13, 30–31,
   50, 51, 54, 78–9, 135,
   137, 143, 144, 145
Africa, 29, 31, 34, 36, 45, 49,
   129 *see also* names of
   countries
Al-Qa'ida, 85, 95, 102, 117,
   129, 137, 140
Algeria, xix, 49, 50, 62, 91,
   94–5, 113, 127, 144
Ali, Rashid, 52, 66
'Ali (Hijaz King), 106
America *see* United States
Anatolia, xvi, 30 *see also*
   Turkey
apostasy, 34–5
   as capital offense, 35, 48
   charge brought against
      Salman Rushdie, 48, 120
   and Muslim rulers, 21, 35,
      115, 116
Arabia
   history, xvi, xxvi–xxviii,
      103
   and imperialism, 50
   as Muslim Holy Land,
      xxvi–xxvii
   no Arabic word for, xix–xx

perceived grievances and
   threats to, xxviii–xxix
US presence in, xxix, 37,
   137
*see also* Saudi Arabia
Arabic language, and modern
   nation-state names,
   xix–xx
al-Assad, Hafiz, 93, 94
Assassins (Muslim sect), 123,
   124, 129
Atatürk, Mustafa Kemal, xvi
Azerbaijan, 76, 84

Baghdad, 38, 137
Baghdad Pact, 84
Barbary corsairs, 45
Ba'th Party, 60, 101, 144
Bayet, Gen. Aubert du, 56
Bazargan, Mehdi, 72
bin Laden, Usama
   and caliphate, xvii
   and Crusades, 41, 134
   messages, xv, xxii–xxv,
      xxix, 27, 134–6, 138–9
   perception of history, xxii
   and Islam, 117
   triggers for action, 37, 137
   view of Bush, xxii, 116
   view of Soviet Union, 54

Bonaparte, Napoleon, 47
Bosnia, 12, 78
Britain
   faces terrorist movements
      in Middle Eastern
      dependencies, 125
   imperialism in Middle East,
      47, 49, 51, 62
   recognizes Saudi kingdom,
      107
Brzezinski, Zbigniew, 72
Bush, George, 52
Bush, George W., xv, xxii,
   116, 133
Byzantine Empire, 29–30, 44

Caesar, 5, 6
caliphate
   abolition of, xvii
   conquests by, 29, 38
   early caliphs, 6, 37–8, 122
   origin of term *caliph*, xvii
   role in Middle Eastern
      history, xvi–xvii, xxvi,
      44, 137
Carter, Jimmy, 64
Caucasus, 48, 75, 127
Chechens, 13, 79, 135
Christianity
   American missionaries, 58
   approach to war, 121–2
   Christians expelled from
      Arabia, xxvii
   in European Middle Ages,
      29–30, 44
   and Islam, 3–9, 14–15,
      37–40, 121–2, 136–7
   *see also* Crusades
Churchill, Winston, 61
Clinton, Bill, 94

Columbus, Christopher, 55
Constantinople, xv, 30, 38
Constantine, 5
crusade, defined, 32 *see also*
   Crusades
Crusades
   capture of Jerusalem, 41,
      42, 43
   defined, 30
   as imperialism, 44
   interest of Muslims in, 41,
      43–4
   jihad compared with, 31–2

Declaration of the World
   Islamic Front for Jihad
   against the Jews and the
   Crusaders, xxii–xxv,
   xxix
democracy, 88, 96, 101, 112,
   139–40, 143–4, 146
*dhimma*, 39
*dīnār*, 37–8
Divan of Jihad Affairs, 31
Dome of the Rock, 37, 38
Dubayet, Gen. Aubert, 56
Dutch imperialism, 45, 49,
   51

East Asia, 97
Egypt
   as birthplace of several
      Sept. 11 terrorists, 102
   conquest by Muslims, 16,
      29
   in Declaration of the World
      Islamic Front for Jihad
      against the Jews and the
      Crusaders, xxiv
   Divan of Jihad Affairs, 31

economic performance, 98,
    101
and imperialism, 47, 49,
    50, 62
national identity issue,
    16–17
overthrow of monarchy, 62
ruler Muhammad 'Ali
    Pasha, 31
and Sayyid Qutb, 65–8
and Soviet Union, 76, 77,
    78, 83
state-sponsored Islamism
    in, 20

Far East, 101
Faraj, 'Abd al-Salām, 115–16
Farsi, xx–xxi
fatwas, xxv, 48, 118–21
fidayeen, 123–4
Frederick II, 43
France, 47, 49, 51, 56–7, 62
fundamentalism see Islamic
    fundamentalism

Germany, 51–2, 59–60, 81,
    127
globalization, 97
Gorbachev, Mikhail, 52
Great Satan, 69, 74, 139
Greeks, 15–16
Gulf War of 1991
    and American Middle East
        policy, 86
    bin Laden view, xxii, xxvi,
        137
    impact on Palestinians, 53
    Muslim view of American
        troops, xxix, 37
    and regime change in Iraq,
        92–3
    Western view, xxv–xxvi

hadīth, 27–8, 131
Hama, 93
Hamas, 130, 134
Hijaz, xxvi, xxvii, 41, 42,
    103, 106–8
Hijra, 28–9
Hindu Kush, 30–31
Hitler, Adolph, 51, 52
Hizbullah, 130
Holocaust, 132
Holy Law see shari'a (Holy
    Law)
holy war see jihad
House of Covenant, 36
House of Islam, 27, 48
House of Jihad, 31
House of Saud, xxviii, 103–4
House of Truce, 36
House of War, 27, 36, 139
human rights, 13, 90, 91–2,
    139
Hurgronje, Snouck, 51
Hussein, Saddam, xxvi, 42,
    53, 60, 74, 85, 87, 92,
    93, 95, 102
Hussein (Hijaz King), 106
al-Husseini, Hajj Amin, 51

Ibn 'Abd al-Wahhab,
    Muhammad, 103, 105
Ibn al-Athir, 43
Ibn Rashid, 106
Ibn Saud, 105–6, 106–7,
    107–8, 109
imperialism
    after end of Cold War, 52–3
    British, 47, 49, 51, 62

Crusades as, 44
defined, 30
Dutch, 45, 49, 51
role in Islamic history,
47–50, 75
Russian, 48, 51, 75, 76, 77,
83
India, 13, 49, 107, 127
infidels, xxi, xxix, 19, 35, 116
see also Crusades
Iran, 22, 50, 51, 62–4, 76, 84,
88, 101 see also Iran-Iraq
war; Iranian Revolution
Iran-Iraq war, xxi–xxii, 13,
80, 129–30
Iranian Revolution
democratic opposition,
139–40
impact in Muslim world,
17–18
and Khomeini, 17, 69,
71–4, 118–21, 139
as popular movement, 20
and shah, 21, 64–5, 89
tyrannical leadership issue,
89–90
US as Great Satan, 69, 74,
139
US hostage crisis, 71–2,
138
Iraq
American policy toward,
86, 87, 92, 143–4
Ba'th Party, 60, 101, 144
as center of Islamic world,
xxvi, 137
in Declaration of the World
Islamic Front for Jihad
against the Jews and the
Crusaders, xxiv

democratic opposition,
140–41
governance, 52, 60, 62, 66,
83, 84, 87, 91, 145
as medieval province, xix
origin of entity, xvi
pro-Nazi regime, 52, 60, 66
see also Gulf War of 1991;
Hussein, Saddam; Iran-
Iraq war
Islam
and Christianity, 3–9,
14–15, 37–40, 121–2,
136–7
conquests in early cen-
turies, 29
dual character, 3, 5–6, 9, 17
elements of hatred and violence, 21–3
and 'enemies of God',
22–3, 59
as leading world civilization during European
dark ages, 3–4, 25, 44
as one of the world's great
religions, 21
in political realm, 11–17
revolutionary wave, 18–21
role of history in modern
Middle East, xxvii–xxii
teaching in Wahhabi-spon-
sored schools, 110–11
tolerance of other religions,
38–9
see also jihad; Islamic fundamentalism; radical
Islam; shari'a
Islamabad, 71
Islamic fundamentalism
as alternative name for

radical Islamism, 20
as alternative to pan-
  Arabism, 113–16
forms of extremism,
  117–18
terminology, 112–13
use of sacred texts, 118
see also radical Islamism
Islamic Salvation Front (FIS),
  94–5
Islamist movements see
  radical Islamism
Israel
  Arab-Israel conflicts, 77,
    79–81, 128, 130
  creation of State of Israel,
    82
  economic performance,
    101
  strategic relationship with
    US, 83–4, 85
  see also Jews

jāhiliyya, 68
Jedda, Saudi Arabia, xxviii,
  12, 106, 107
Jerusalem
  in Declaration of the World
    Islamic Front for Jihad
    against the Jews and the
    Crusaders, xxix, xxv
  Dome of the Rock, 37, 38
  history during Crusades,
    41–2, 43
Jesus Christ, 5, 9, 30
Jews
  blamed for September 11
    attacks, 133
  in Declaration of the World
    Islamic Front for Jihad

against the Jews and the
  Crusaders, xxiv
expelled from Arabia, xxvii
see also Israel
jihad
  against apostates, 34–5
  as armed struggle, 25,
    26–36
  as bequeathed by Muham-
    mad, 25–6
  Crusades compared with,
    31–2
  Declaration of the World
    Islamic Front for Jihad
    against the Jews and the
    Crusaders, xxii–xxv,
    xxix
  history of, 28–31
  as moral striving, 25, 26,
    31
  offensive and defensive,
    26–7, 29–30
  origin of term, 25
  in Qur'an, 25–6, 27
  role of martyrs, 32–3
  role of truces, 36, 38
  rules of warfare, 28, 33–6
jizya, 36, 39
Jordan, xvi, 41, 83, 84

Khomeini, Ayatollah, 7, 17,
  69, 71–4, 118–21, 139
Khrushchev, Nikita, 82
Kurds, 92
Kuwait, xxv, xxvi, xxix, 53,
  98, 99, 100

League of Nations, 49
Lebanon, xvi, 60, 83, 84, 93,
  100, 101, 130, 138

Libya, xix, 88, 90, 99, 102

*madrasas*, 110
martyrs, 32–3
Marxism, 60–61
Mecca, xxvi, 10, 28, 29, 71, 103, 106
Medina, xxvi, 6, 10, 28, 38, 103, 106
Middle East
  American complicity with corrupt rulers, 65, 69, 81, 89–96, 102
  beginning of modern history, 47
  economic performance, 97–101
  imperialism in, 30, 44, 47–50, 51, 52–3, 75–6, 83
  rise of anti-Americanism, 59–69, 74–5, 81, 136
  role of Islamic history, xviii–xxii
  Western expectations, 90–96
  *see also* Muslims
modernity *see* modernization
modernization
  desire for, 102
  effects of, 50
  excessive, 115
  failure of, 97–102
  and oil, 111–12
  as the problem, 102, 103, 115
Morocco, 12, 49, 56, 64
Mosaddeq, Mohammed, 62–4
mosques, xxv, 7, 20

mufti, 10, 11, 119
Mufti of Jerusalem, 51, 66
Muhammad, Prophet
  creation of Islamic political and religious community, 3–4, 5–6, 9
  dual aspects of his career, 10, 23
  insults as offense against, 119–21
  and jihad, 25–8, 28–9
  relationship to Arabia, xxvi, xxvii
Muhammad 'Ali Pasha, 31
murder, 34, 121, 122–4, 131–2 *see also* suicide
Muslim Brothers, 65, 68, 93, 94, 112, 128
Muslims
  economic statistics, 97–101
  as minority population, 13, 140
  temptations of democracy, 139
  view of leaders as apostates, 21, 35, 115, 116
  *see also* Islam; Middle East

Najd, region of Arabia, 103, 106
al-Nasser, Gamal 'Abd, 66, 78, 83, 84, 101
Nebuchadnezzar, 42
Netherlands, imperialism, 45, 49, 51
Nubia, 36

oil, xxviii, 19, 58, 62–3, 86, 108–9, 112
Organization of the Islamic

Conference (OIC),
    12–14, 64, 68–9, 79, 139
Ottoman Empire
    decline and defeat, xv–xvi,
        xix, 45, 49, 104, 105
    rule of, 11, 30, 31, 44–5,
        56, 103–4

Pakistan, xxi, 20, 71, 129
Palestine
    conquest by Muslims, 29
    division into two segments,
        xvi
    Israel-Palestine conflict,
        53–4, 79–81, 128, 134
    Jews in, xxvii, 82, 125
    as name from classical
        antiquity, xix
    and OIC, 13, 79
    origin of entity, xvi
Palestine Liberation Organ-
    ization (PLO), 53–4, 79,
    124, 126–7
pan-Islamism, 127–8
Persia, xx–xxi, 29, 47, 76 see
    also Iran
Pharoah, xxii, 10, 116
poll-tax, 36, 39

Qaddafi, Mu'ammar, 102
Qatar, 98, 99
qadi, 10, 11
Al-Quds al-'Arabi (news-
    paper), xxii
Qu'ran, 7, 25–6, 27, 37, 39,
    69, 118–21, 145
Qutb, Sayyid, 65–8, 69

radical Islamism
    as attack on its own rulers

and leaders, 20–21, 115,
    116
and democracy, 96
and 'enemies of God',
    22–3, 59
forms of extremism, 20–21,
    117–18
    see also Iranian Revolution
Raffarin, Jean-Pierre, 42
Reagan, Ronald, 138
Red Army, 54
religion see Christianity;
    Islam
revolution, defined, 18 see
    also Iranian Revolution
Reynald of Châtillon, 41–2,
    43
Riyadh, Saudi Arabia, xxviii,
    104
Roman Empire, 5, 6, 9
Rushdie, Salman, 48, 118–21
Russia, 13, 30, 44, 47, 48, 51,
    75, 76–7, 83 see also
    Soviet Union

Sabra and Shatila, 93–4
Sadat, Anwar, 21, 48, 52, 74,
    78, 115, 116
Said, Nuri, 83
Saladin, 42–3
Satan see Great Satan
Saudi Arabia
    changes brought by oil,
        xxviii, 109–11
    contrasted with countries
        affected by imperialism,
        50
    in Declaration of the World
        Islamic Front for Jihad
        against the Jews and the

Crusaders, xxiii, xxiv,
    xxix
economic performance, 98
flag, 35–6
history, xvi, xxviii, 103–8
and House of Saud, xxviii,
    103–4
as member of UN Human
    Rights Commission, 90
name, xix–xx
and radical Islamism, 20,
    102
and Palestinians, 53
US troops in, xxix, 37, 137
Selaniki Mustafa Efendi, 46
September 11 attacks, 102,
    129, 131–4
shah of Iran, 21, 62, 63, 64–5,
    89
*shahīd*, 32–3
shari'a (Holy Law)
converting to and from
    Islam, 48
defined, 7
and fatwas, 119–21
and jihad, 26–7, 28, 33–6
role of ulema, 8
and terrorism, 34
tolerance of other religions,
    38–9
Shi'a, 92
Slade, Adolphus, 50
slaves and slavery, 34, 36, 50
socialism, 61
Somalia, 13, 138
Soviet Union
and Afghanistan, 13, 54,
    78–9, 135, 137
arms deal with Egypt, 76, 83
collapse of, 52, 53, 54, 137

and creation of State of
    Israel, 82
interests in Middle East, 51,
    52, 60–61, 75–8, 82, 83
recognizes Saudi kingdom,
    107
Spain, 29, 30, 44, 55, 99
Stalin, Josef, 82
Standard Oil of California,
    108–9
Sudan, xxiv, 13, 88, 90, 91
Suez War of 1956, 82
suicide, in Islam, 33, 124,
    130–31, 145
Syria
Ba'th Party, 60, 101, 144
conquest by Muslims, 29
division into two segments,
    xvi
economic performance,
    100, 101
Hama uprising, 93
and human rights, 90, 91
Jews in, xxvii
as name from classical
    antiquity, xix
origin of entity, xvi
and Soviet Union, 83
Vichy-controlled, 52, 60

al-Tahtawi, Rifa'a Rafi', 57
*takfīr*, 48
Taliban, xxi, 112
TASS, 107–8
Tatars (*also* Tartars), 13, 30,
    44
Tehran, 63, 72, 119, 123, 138
terrorism
Al-Qaida, 85, 95, 102, 117,
    129, 137, 140

and innocent bystanders,
125, 128–9
and Islamic holy law, 34
global dimensions to, 146
nationalist motives, 125–7
phases of, 125–9
religious motives, 127–8
rise of, 117–40
suicide terrorists, 33,
129–31, 145
*see also* September 11
attacks
Third Reich, 52, 60, 66
Tunisia, xix, 49
Turkey
adoption of name, xx
democratic institutions,
101, 139, 146
and discovery of America,
55
economic performance, 98
as independent, 50, 51
liberation of, xvi
as member of OIC, 12
Soviet threat to, 76, 84
Turks, xxi, 15–16, 30, 45, 47,
48, 76, 77, 110

ulema, xxv, 7–8
'Umar (caliph), xx, xxvi–xxvii
Umayyad caliphs, 36
unbelievers, 34–5, 36, 136–7
*see also* infidels
United Arab Emirates, 98, 99,
100
United Nations, 78–9, 82, 90
United States
American Revolution,
55–6, 57, 75
early descriptions in Arab

world, 55–8
and imperialism, 52–3
military intervention in
Middle East, 143–4
perceived complicity with
corrupt Middle East gov-
ernments, 65, 69, 81,
89–96, 102
rise of anti-Americanism in
Middle East, 59–69,
74–5, 81, 136
strategic relationship with
Israel, 83–4, 85
troops in Saudi Arabia,
xxix, 37, 137
way of life, 58, 67–8, 69,
136, 139
'Uthman (caliph), 122

Wahhabism, xxviii, 103–11,
112
Westernizers, 113, 115
Wolff, Heinrich, 51
women, 35, 50, 92, 130, 136
World Trade Center *see* September 11 attacks

Zahedi, General Fazlollah, 63